Jim Klobuchar

Pursued by Grace

A Newspaperman's Own Story
of Spiritual Recovery

Augsburg
MINNEAPOLIS

PURSUED BY GRACE
A Newspaperman's Own Story of Spiritual Recovery

Scripture is from the Revised Standard Version of the Bible, copyright © 1989 by the Division of Christian Education of the National Council of the Churches of Christ in the U.S.A. and used by permission.

Cover photo by John Palumbo.
Cover design by David Meyer.
Text design by James Satter.

Library of Congress Cataloging-in-Information Data

Klobuchar, Jim.
    Pursued by grace : a newspaperman's own story of recovery / Jim Klobuchar.
        p.   cm.
    ISBN 0-8066-3649-1 (alk. paper)
    1. Klobuchar, Jim. 2. Christian biography—United States.
I. Title.
BR1725.K55A3   1998
277.3'0825'092—dc21
[b]   98-28754
                                              CIP

Manufactured in the U.S.A.   AF 9-3649

02   01   00   5   6   7   8   9   10

*This is for Al Anderson, a Samaritan I came to love,
and for all of the other Samaritans in my life, those I know,
those I will never know*

Contents

A Cry from a Lonely Room

I heard a condemnation that gave me no escape. It left me dazed and shaken as I crossed the hall to my room in a small chemical-dependency treatment center in the Minnesota countryside. Several men and women I knew distantly, fellow clients, passed me in the hallway. We usually nodded. On this day I didn't see their faces, didn't hear their voices.

The condemnation was my own. It was as though I'd been thrust into a sound studio and forced to watch a film of the last thirty years of my life, secretly made, frame by frame, revealing a person I'd never seen and a destruction I couldn't have imagined. Its cost in emotional injury to those closest to me, its cost in broken relationships and violated trust piled up with each frame of revelation until I found myself looking at it with a shame so painful that I wanted to scream at myself in the mirror: "How could you have done this?"

But I avoided the mirror, and it wasn't a movie I saw. It was a blackboard that chronicled the wreckage of a part of my life, and the wreckage that I'd inflicted on the lives of others over the years in a rampage of self-gratification. It had been me first, a chase, renewable daily. I piled my energies and ingenuities into it—my bag, my pace, my thrills. I'd ignored the cost. I'd refused to make the moral assessments. I refused because the other side of my life was filled with excitement and strokes from achieving and with perpetual motion.

But on this day in the country I was confronted for the first time with the full weight of the injury the chase had caused. When I got to my room, I closed the door to escape into aloneness. But privacy gave me no relief. No amount of self-accusation did, nor the taking on of guilt. The numbness in my body couldn't dissolve the shame. Finally, I knelt, helpless to do any more.

"God help me," I said.

I expected no answer.

But one came.

It was a beginning.

The suggestion for this book came from a friend who spent most of his working years as a publisher in religion and spirituality. Both of these, he remarked mischievously, seemed to come hard to me. I found that amusing and accurate. When he also suggested that I might perform a service by sharing some of the bruising track I've been on—trying to get comfortable with faith, trying to find faith, in fact—the jocularity disappeared. Pain and the discovery and eventual confession of wholesale self-deception in our lives tend to be a serious business. So does separation from God. That has been the place where I've been for most of life despite my distress and guilt over it and despite my struggles to break out of it into the clearer air of belief.

I can't know if or how my struggles mirror those of others, including those who read this book. I'd guess many of us share a common history of battling dilemmas, trying to puzzle out the riddles of who and what God is, envying (sometimes awed by) people around us who seem untroubled by such doubts. We have been hauled in opposite directions by our devotion to logic, which shuns mysteries, and by our intuitive need to believe in a benign and supernatural power in our lives, more simply called grace and God.

Most people have to deal with doubts. Mine seemed to have acquired a pretty high level of virulence and a long life. But I've been impelled by a stubborn need throughout the years to move beyond those confusions and to make some decisions, to invite something better into my life that would bring me to a point where the dilemmas are resolved. I felt the need because the confusions and the arrogance that came with them, partly fed by alcohol during some of those years, frankly were killing me, and not so quietly. My efforts to reach a reconciliation are set out here in this brief chronicle. Whether they are able serve the needs of others is something that must be left to the reader, and the higher wisdom of the late Al Anderson who encouraged me to share my story, and whose counsel, goodwill, and friendship helped save my life.

1

Hearing God in the Thunder

Trying to meet God in the mining town where I grew up was a hair-raising walk through the graveyards of the child's imagination. We connected God with death and fright. There weren't many hallelujahs.

The sound and face of God meshed with the quake of cave-ins in the underground iron mines and the melancholy of the funerals that followed. The signals that God was on the scene were emergency sirens at the minehead and, in church, the thunderclaps of threatened damnation that flavored the Sunday pulpit styles of the times. They mingled with the folk mythology that the immigrant elders stirred into their religion. A storm would send its volatile clouds racing across the northern Minnesota sky. Lightning split the gloaming. And my Slovenian grandmother, much venerated by the family's children, would explain the rumbling in tones of hushed gravity: *"Bogitz!"* God (is speaking)!

So God lived in the sky, and thunder was his hard judgment or warning. Of what? My grandmother never explained. I couldn't follow her Balkan syntax at the time, but I know now that what she was saying, *"Ce ne bos poreden, bogitz bo shtrafuh,"* was hard-core immigrant theology spliced with some old-fashioned behavior management: If you don't straighten out, God will deal with you. Grandmothers in the mining town took their roles seriously. They were the designated interpreters of God's noisy ultimatums. I think my grandmother really believed it, that God was bellowing his displeasure with thunder from the sky.

And if she did, I wasn't going to quarrel with the theology. My grandmother was the matriarch of our family. She was a squat little empress with strong hands roughened by hours of punching the clumpy earth of Minnesota's Iron Range with her garden hoe. She bent over it with her babushka snapping in the wind, her apron hanging to her ankles, shoes sinking in the soil beneath the pole beans that were the pride of her cultivations. She was a gnome puttering in the dirt, but she prized this work of providing the winter stores of bottled vegetables that were the staples of her household in the Great Depression.

The sight in my childhood always gave me a smile when I'd make the voyage to her house from two blocks down the road. Because I was her first grandchild I occupied a special if undeclared seat in her affections. To me she was some kind of homegrown Mother Hubbard with that blowing babushka, but although I didn't know the word then, the respect I felt for her never wavered. We loved her, I loved her, with reason. In most things she was wise. In family matters she was the intercessor and the healer. When she came in from the garden, she'd change clothes, wash, sit at her kitchen table, offer me a large slice of warm buttered bread fresh from her oven and say, "Jeemy, sit here; we talk; all right?" Her face glowed beneath her black and silver hair. She'd touch my face, her reddened hands now tender and her round face full of invitation. Her English was awkward, but it didn't embarrass her and it certainly didn't embarrass me. She talked about school and helping my mother. But for all these moments of gentleness, she was still the empress. She decided the right of road in the family and pretty much what was on God's mind.

And usually what was on God's mind was, as it filtered to the impressionable kid of the mining town, not far from grief and punishment.

In this and other ways, from my early catechism to the underground fatalities that were dramatized by the sight of a funeral catafalque standing in the aisle of the church, God scared the socks off me. A hundred times in later years I was tempted to blame those early pictures of a stern and uncompromising God for the emotional disasters and spiritual wandering of my adulthood. You may have done the same. My attempts were always phony.

The northern Minnesota mine country of my boyhood was a place that Carl Sandburg might have found even better suited for his biceps-and-blood poetry than his hog-butchering Chicago. The Iron Range was and is a land of immigrant sweat and dreams. For more than a half-century, its underground tunnels and the caverns of its open pits poured millions of tons of high-grade ore into the molten pools of America's steel vats. It drew immigrants by the thousands, dark-haired, sausage-eating Slavs from the Balkans; blue-eyed, fish-eating Finns and Norwegians and Swedes from Scandinavia; Italians, Bulgarians, Greeks, and the rest, most of them from southern Europe. They came with few illusions. To make a living they were going to have to tear the ore out of the earth, and some of them would die doing it. They came with their Old World enmities and feuds, and for at least two generations a Catholic marrying a Methodist or Presbyterian was considered right on the margin of violating natural law. A Lutheran marrying a Catholic was a little better than borderline, but barely.

Yet for those decades of the great immigration at the turn of the century, the culture of Minnesota's Iron Range, the hunger of the ethnic clans to make it in America and to see their children educated, was the essence of the American ideal. In a gruff and muscular way, yet oddly lyrical, it united the impatient drive of a burgeoning America with the visions of the immigrant.

It wasn't round-the-clock grimness and hardball. The nationalities brought their songs and quirks and cooking and games, and they fused a rollicking society that was enriched by the marvelous recreation and beauty of the lake and forest country nearby. And they also brought their God. In my hometown of Ely there was a Catholic church, a Methodist church, and a Presbyterian church, as well as the Finnish Lutheran church and another Lutheran church. To make sure the Iron Range was never going to give its soul for conformity, there was also a Holy Roller church.

As a genuflecting, Catholic kid in that town, I was willing to grant the non-Catholic kids an outside chance of reaching heaven. The emissaries of God in my church were the wall-rattling senior pastor, the Reverend Frank Mihelcic, and the coterie of nuns who during summer vacations taught us about the dark destinies of liars, thieves, and the ones who missed mass on Sunday mornings.

Unintentionally, the sisters contributed to the hovering dread I felt when God was re-introduced in the choir loft where we took catechism classes at St. Anthony's. I say unintentionally. Mostly the sisters were sweet and informative and caring. They spoke of a receptive Jesus, of his power to cleanse. They spoke of the qualities of humility and forgiveness, concepts that might not have occurred immediately to an eight-year-old fresh off the ball field. When one Monday morning I recited the week's previous lesson without a break, the sacrifice of Father Damien in the leper colony in the Hawaiian Islands, I was rewarded with a small portrait of Jesus Christ with his hand at his heart. I rushed home to show it and was all but smothered in the most ardent hug of the week by my mother, who was convinced I was home free toward becoming the family's first priest.

No, it wasn't the sisters' philosophy that scared me about God. It was the gloomy garments they wore, the dress code of the times. In summer, the sisters materialized in our town to run the catechism studies, instructed by the bishop of Duluth and our Balkan-born priest to help put us on the road to redemption. This service was intended to insulate us against the time when, after high school, many in our number would go underground to shovel iron ore. There we could be inveigled to drink in support of the town's three dozen liquor joints or otherwise to conduct wastrel lives.

About the demeanor of those well-remembered nuns, I want now to amend the record. A few of them were stiff and formidable, in tone with the popular parodies of today's comedy theaters. But most of them taught with wit and benevolence and a working knowledge of the slang of the time. Yet until you knew that, the sisters' appeared to be the forerunners of doom to an eight-year-old kid. Their clothes seemed drawn from the cloak room of the Inquisition. They wore black gowns and cowls, and around their necks clung fluted white ruffles that pinched their jaws and cheeks and seemed to bleach their skin paler than it was. When they talked about martyrs and the penalties for sin, the atmospherics in the choir loft tended to get pretty somber. Maybe they should have. I remember the day we learned about Jesus Christ deputizing the apostles as confessors. Over the railing of the choir balcony, beyond the pipe organ that Mary Hutar played so vigorously at Sunday mass, our glances could not escape the front of the aisle near the altar, which had been prepared for the funeral of an iron miner killed in an accident at 1,500 feet below the surface three days before. It was where our fathers were working at that moment. It was where some in our class would work the rest of their adult lives, where others—I was among them—would work in the summer months to raise money for college. God was in the choir loft. He was presiding over the confession of sin in the curtained boxes of the sanctuary below us. God was present at the head of the aisle, where a dead miner would receive his last rites. The smell of God was the incense whose fumes the priest spread above the coffin from an urn he swung by a gold chain at the requiem mass. The candles burned red in their votive cups, and the red flames were a summons to God. So God came in a spray of incense and by red candlelight, in the presence of death. A God of doom.

We were too young to understand the cleansing power of confession and contrition and the surmounting beauty of a

God loving and forgiving and gracing those he had created. We were not mature enough to appreciate the sublimity of the sacrifice that was celebrated in the worship service. The deliverance should have been on the day we received our first communion. And I would never minimize the power of that moment, the feeling of unity with Jesus I felt on that day, walking to my parents in my white suit and tie after the service, a flower in my breast pocket. I felt that union because as a boy I was truly aroused by the idea of worship, by the idea of searching for goodness, by the idea of heaven. Heaven as what? Heaven as a reward for goodness.

The idea of unconditional grace bestowed by God was years away for me. But no matter how I understood it, or didn't understand it, there was beyond all dispute a grace suffusing my life on the day of my first communion. Jesus was with me. I had received his body and blood. We are inseparable.

I felt it. I still feel it each time I receive Communion.

And yet apart from hours such as those, most of us when we were growing up identified God—or at least I did—with mourning and death and punishment. It was an unreasonably rough rap on God. The austerity wasn't much relieved when Father Mike revved up in the pulpit.

Frank Mihelcic was the head pastor of the church but in appearance seemed better cast as the head meat cutter in a turn-of-the-century butcher shop. He had a powerful, thick-set body and a round, meaty face spread bountifully about a pug nose. He was an immigrant from what became Yugoslavia before the country's ultimate dismemberment. Dozens of his parishioners in the early and middle century were either Slovenian or Croatian immigrants or their sons and daughters, almost all of them fluent in the Yugoslavian languages. Frank Mihelcic waged aggressive war against the devil multilingually, in his native Slovenian and in a denser but still fervid English. When he was out of earshot, the flock called him Father Mike. That couldn't have wounded his feelings. Mike sounded like a name that belonged in the ore pits.

It was abrupt and demanded attention, which largely characterized the reverend's pulpit style. He was a booming autocrat when he went on the attack, hurling his indictments with equal rage against backsliding on the road to heaven and bashfulness at collection time.

My hometown was essentially a frontier town. It was clumped around the skeletal towers of the mining headframes and the mountains of ore tailings, but gentled by the nearness of the hundreds of lakes and streams and the great fir groves of semi-wilderness around it. Because it was a place that demanded strong hands to bore into the earth for its vermilion treasure, we expected no honed oratory from the pulpit. Father Mike was appalled by the raw stamina of some of his penitents in the liquor joints on Saturday night. His assaults on these habits were strident and without mercy. They did nothing to kindle thoughts of a charitable God. His voice rose in fury when he talked about God's displeasure, creating a picture of long and incendiary nights in hell. You could almost hear the wails of the damned screened through Father Mike's roaring oratory.

To the kids, Father Mike was mostly a paper tiger because it was easy to laugh at his storming in the pulpit, and he couldn't badger the kids at collection time. So we got along. But confirmation was a time when Father Mike decided his tutorial powers were under public scrutiny by the bishop. At St. Anthony's Church, confirmation was as elective as the military draft in World War II. The confirmation classes filled at least the first ten pews in the church, and graduation was a big deal. The bishop from Duluth, Thomas Welch, would come to preside and ceremonially interrogate the confirmands to determine their level of readiness to go out into the world to take on the devil. It may have been a pro forma exercise for the bishop, but it was a moment burdened with crisis for Father Mike. While the bishop carried out the inquiry with his back to the altar, Father Mike sat behind him, candidly coaching the scholars with body language and silent mouthings when one of them was stumped. Toward the end, when one of them completely flunked out on a question of when was the Pope infallible—"when teaching on matters of faith or morals"—Father Mike worked his lips into a mortified "you dummy."

Yet when he talked one-to-one with those in his congregation who were grieving, or with the victims of alcoholic behavior, or with the lonely, Frank Mihelcic was capable of an unmistakable compassion and emotion. My mother told of a scene after a requiem mass, of Father Mike embracing the parents of a young man who'd died in the town's hospital, a youngster who'd been one of his pupils in Sunday school. The tough-shelled priest prayed quietly for a few moments to comfort the couple. Father Mike the healer. And then his lips began to tremble in the grief he was sharing. He seemed about to excuse himself, my mother said, but recovered and asked the couple to kneel with him. They prayed together, hand-in-hand, strengthening each other.

Admitting his vulnerability on his knees, Father Mike was a bigger man, a better servant, than he was shouting in the pulpit. My mother didn't say that. I don't know that I would have read the scene that way then.

I would today.

To a youngster seeing this other face of the religion he preached, it would have removed some of the overlying dread. Maybe the English language in the liturgy would have helped, although I still remember fondly Father Mike's deep Slavic baritone chanting that mysterious Latin after a prayer: *Per omnia saecula saeculorum.* Maybe it would have helped to know what he was singing: "This is for all ages, unending."

What a lovely invocation. But in the light of years of groping to track God in my turmoil of later times—to accept and believe—I recognize now a far more damaging blind spot. What I didn't see then, because she was so near, was my model for believing in a sheltering and intimate God, one to whom I could give absolute trust. In the house, my mother rarely reflected a fear of God. She made no show of her spiritual life. In her bedroom she hung a small crucifix above the bed, and in the den a picture of Jesus praying in the Garden of Gethsemane. That was it. No more icons. She didn't preach religion in the house and, although she was disturbed by my father's indifference toward Sunday mass, she would attend every Sunday at eight o'clock, walking the mile through snowstorms when she had to, reciting her beads, signing herself with holy water.

What she did every Sunday was to thank God for our health and to pray for her children and her husband. Her belief was quiet, humble, and unbreakable. Her only gesture as an evangelist in the house was to prod my brother and me, on the day the school year began, to kneel and ask for guidance. We did, not so much to please God as to placate our mother. She believed that prayers would be answered. She prayed that my father would end his Saturday night drinking sprees and return to church by her side.

In his mid-forties, my father ended his Saturday night drinking sprees. He joined the Knights of Columbus and, each week thereafter, received Holy Communion at my mother's side.

Her campaign for her oldest son took longer.

I started to drift after confirmation. The sermons bored me. The hymns sounded too solemn. I left home for mass each Sunday morning but began detouring to the Ely News Store to read a magazine or drink a malt. When my mother asked about the priest's sermon, I finessed it by saying the priest helped me understand the gospel, which sounded acceptable to her. So in addition to breaking the sabbath I added deceit to the morning's glossary of delinquency. Within a couple of years, God was pretty much a nonentity in my life. Whatever cover stories I made up to give myself respectability at home simply acted to deepen the deceit and the alienation.

I was the adolescent getting wise, the young adult in transition to a widening world and higher speed. Who needs God? Who is God? What was God? Does this sound familiar? Probably. "Give me some answers," demands the young adult getting wise. Me. I made the demands. But sometime later, about the time I headed for college, the demands sounded less arrogant. I'd stopped going to church, but I didn't have the nerve to let go. Nerve? Maybe it was something else, something more becoming. How about guilt? I remembered my mother's serenity with God, her prayers to Jesus, her unarguing faith. I envied it. I tried going back to church, but it was a fraudulent exercise. I didn't feel it. In the years ahead I started out on a dozen trails. None of them got much past Me.

You might have been there in the same morass, or still are. You will get no doctrinal directions here on finding a more sensible road. What you will find are the lurches and delusions of somebody who would have followed them into the grave except for a confrontation one day in 1993 and a chase that ended in a homely room in a chemical-dependency center in the country. It was there where I felt the touch of a forgiving God once more.

It was also the end of an exploration of a kind you may have been making yourself. I don't think there are any special rules governing where and how we explore. Most of us grapple with the ideas of faith and reconciliation. We dangle by the thumbs of doubt. We often pretend commitment to faith. It's something we want, and it feels good in the résumés of the person we'd like to be and the life we know we ought to be leading. And then we compare it with real commitment, unambiguous and straight from the gut. When we see it, we yearn for it. Maybe "we" is too inclusive. I yearned for it, because it eluded me for decades.

Let me stop right there, because that is one dazzling jewel of self-deception. Faith wasn't doing the eluding; I was. Which takes us into the well-traveled field of hypocrisy. I'd look at the practicing Christians sitting next to me in church, listening to those mossy parables in the Gospels, looking devout but maybe feeling as troubled as the ones who are unconvinced. If that's true, how do they come to grips with the daunting gulf between the professed values of Christianity and their daily behavior? In short, what do you do about being human? How far over the rainbow is a personal peace? How do you finally come together with God, when you want to but can't seem to tell yourself the truth?

How easy is it to confess that my life is centered on me, my goals, my fears, my comfort? Or to admit that what's killing my connection with God is my selfishness?

That's where the needle was stuck for me for most of my life. And then came an encounter when I'd reached my sixty-fourth year, a figure that may have threatened the post-war record for sustained ego. It couldn't have come, I know now, until despair came first. And when it did, I saw no vision and heard no voice. What I saw was truth, my shams and weaknesses and pretensions. What I felt was helplessness and remorse. What I received was acceptance. It didn't happen on any jack pine version of the road to Damascus. It didn't transform my personality or exorcise the demons within me on the spot.

It did leave me mute and drained in the realization of the corruptive power of my dishonesties. But ultimately it reversed much of my behavior and changed the direction of my life. It thrust me into an adventure of the spirit and a discovery I hadn't conceived in a lifetime of prowling mountains and crevasses and besieging bureaucratic fortresses as a newspaperman.

It brought me closer than I had ever been to a personal peace.

It was a moment more visceral than sublime, digging and prodding into my insides rather than my mind or even my soul. It came with pain and disclosure. At the time of my deepest humiliation, I felt moved by a benediction, by a forgiveness for which I was too despondent to ask and by an embrace I had no right to expect.

No, I didn't hear God. If I did, the words might have chided my theology: "What does deserving have to do with all of this?"

At odd times in my life, the voice of Peggy Lee, the pop ballad singer out of the Dakota prairie, gets entwined with my spiritual world. I'm not sure this would have impressed her, but it's the truth. Years ago she recorded a song entitled "Is That All There Is?" It was a languorous, wistful hymn to the futility of life. Each chorus described an incident in her life, culminating with a love affair. All of them fell beneath her expectations and left her empty or unfulfilled. Something was missing in life, which had promised more. When life pretended to deliver excitement, the excitement dissolved. When it pretended to deliver tenderness, the tenderness left in a river of tears. Her response was a shrug and a roguish escape into a manufactured good time. If that's all there is, my friend, she sang in the refrain, "Then let's go on dancing; let's break out the booze and have a ball, if that's all."

If that's all there is, my friend. I might have been tweaked by the artistry with which Peggy Lee sold that song. Or it might have been the funky and bittersweet fatalism of it that stuck the lyrics into the back cells of my mind. The song was saying: "Hope is a pipe dream. Get by without it."

You can, but that makes you less human. Yet the lyrics in that pop tune and their wry solution to life got threaded into my ramblings to look into the face of God in the years that followed.

No, I told myself, that's not all there is. Getting a charge, making it, is not all there is. But that bluntly characterized how I lived for years, knowing better. So I fought with myself and I have to admit now that the title of that song puts us into a broader canvas than the lyricist might have imagined. What do we extract from life? What gives it worth, gives us worth?

In later years I found myself conducting fierce mental brawls with myself on propositions like that. I was the advocate and opponent, arguing all sides with equal zeal and equal puzzlement. It was a one-man show. On long solo approach hikes to a mountain climb I would engage myself in head-splitting debates, ranging from anguish to absurdity. On some stretches of the trail I would actually be talking to myself, out loud. How much do I need a God in my life? I'd say I want him there, and I need him because I'm careening around with no center of constancy in my life. But then I would ask, "Is there such a center and such a power?" God? Does somebody have to prove there is a God?

Once in the Andes, mentally exhausted by one of those intramural struggles, I knelt to pray and ended up annoying a village herdsman who was in a hurry and had no patience with visiting fanatics.

It was one way to gain 3,000 feet. Yet for all of my mystification in this sorting-through process, which has gone on through most of my adult life, the end conclusion usually came down about the same. I have to find a way to believe that God is here. The problem, I would tell myself, is not knowing how to handle that phenomenon. The second problem was not knowing that I didn't have to handle it at all. A small voice perhaps should have told me that: "Accept and go on." What I did know, and what I believe more emphatically now that I have made most of my blunders and some of my atonements, is that human beings are human for a reason that goes beyond the reasoning process. We are human because of something in us, something we have received, that goes beyond our ability to laugh and cry and sympathize, beyond the choices we make and the moons to which we can fly.

If we can create and understand beauty; if we can reflect it; if for all the temptations to greed in our lives and in spite of our random acts of selfishness, we can recognize the needs of others and feed and clothe them; if we can perform acts of sacrifice and nurture love, there is something more than goodness or the potential for goodness in us. There is divinity.

I now believe that. That belief hasn't spared me those private bouts of anguish-and-doubt. But if we all had undiluted faith and sureness, most of the preachers would be unemployed, and most of the confession boxes would be empty.

The searcher asks: "Is it all right to believe, or try to believe, and still be curious and marginally baffled?" This is serious business to the seeker. What do you do about ambivalence or, in fact, about human weakness? Here is a man who today prostrates himself in contrition for some vile behavior of his. Asking for forgiveness brings him closer to God. He feels purged. Blessed. But tomorrow, when the guilt of his behavior has receded, he's not so sure about all that business of humility and prostration.

Is he a hypocrite? Sure. Who isn't? He's also fallibly human.

He's one of us. Scared, muddling, wanting to get closer to God and to feel God's benevolence. How's he going to reach that place, if he reaches it at all? Is there a trail somewhere in this forest?

The forest can get deep. Let's walk deeper.

2

Good-bye, God, but Leave Some of Your Ornaments

Pope Pius XII was going to appear in five minutes. A polyglot audience of several thousand prepared for him noisily in their bleacher seats at his palatial retreat outside Rome, steadily working themselves toward an advanced stage of euphoria.

To a corporal in the U.S. Army in 1952, geared for something more sedate, the scene had the raise-the-roof feel of a high-school basketball tournament. It generated the same electric lilt and colliding sound waves of the dueling chants I remembered from the years when the student bodies from a half-dozen Minnesota mining towns stoked up the arena. "Two bits, four bits, six bits, a dollar, Everybody from Aurora stand up and holler." All right, the yells are zingier in the high-school gyms of today. This was the early 1950s, when the town elders tried to keep the lid on.

One difference between the pope's claque and the basketball crowd was that these folks carried rosaries and wore big buttons inscribed with fishes. From one section of the gallery, a delegation of more than five hundred bus riders from Spain launched their syncopation. It had an exuberant stop-and-go staccato that rattled off the walls of the solemn stone architecture of the papal fortress at Castel Gandolfo in the Alban

Hills south of Rome, the summer home of the pope away from the Vatican. The Spanish chant shook up the blood of the American corporal. I had no clue to the lyrics. But the rhythm yanked me back to those high-school bleachers where the contagion rolled through the amphitheater and whipped up the crowd with one of the favorite yells of impending victory. I'd gotten over the awkwardness of being a loner at Castel Gandolfo, and, sitting in one of the Italian enclaves, I loosened up and joined the Spaniards' locomotive chant with my own lyrics: "Our team is red hot."

The Italians in my section were marshaling their own forces and nobody heard my alien sounds. If they did, they paid no notice. In another gallery the crowd from Bologna sang its salutes in a round. The Portuguese in the adjacent section horned in. Signs identifying the cities and countries bobbed in the crowd. The chanting rose and surged through the courtyard like ocean breakers. Someplace in the jubilant din I heard voices in English, but they dissolved in the tide of Italian vowels. I was sitting with a bunch from Portofina, folks who tried their level best to extend their hospitality to the uniformed American corporal in their midst. Because I was well and truly engulfed by the fraternity of the crowd, I tried to get into the chant of the Portofinans. But it felt dumb, so I just listened and swayed with the others.

Suddenly the crowd erupted in full voice, because here was the Pope, the Holy Father of the Roman Catholic Church and its millions, the direct successor to the big fisherman, Peter himself. Pius XII materialized on the balcony in his light summer robes and skull cap and his brittle, ascetic face. Acknowledging the cheers, he smiled and worked his hands gracefully in cadence, palms and fingers cupped, giving a blessing and then addressing his greeting in all available languages. His English was brief and thick and all but incomprehensible. But this was the man we were taught was infallible when teaching matters of faith and morals, and because this day was one of those feasts of friendship and commitment, nobody much cared about the words. At the end we prayed, thousands of voices in mixed languages, a congregation celebrating its universality.

The child in me trembled. Back home, when I'd entered the great university in hot pursuit of truth, determined to cast off the hobgoblins of superstition, I sometimes smiled, remembering those indoctrination sessions of the sisters in catechism. But here were thousands of voices singing their declaration of belief, identifying their unbreakable community of faith, led in prayer by a man whose presence linked this moment with the charter given by Jesus Christ himself. Which meant, for them, Jesus Christ was there.

As the crowd dispersed, a certain numbness crept over me. I walked toward the railroad station, not quite understanding whether for me this was some kind of transformation or whether I'd been willingly overwhelmed by the fervor of the crowd and the power of history. One thing was for sure, I hadn't thought of the church of my childhood—the one presided over by the God of dread—creating this scene of frenzied joy.

I boarded the train feeling vaguely sanctified. But I might better have asked, "What am I doing here?"

"What am I doing here when I have given up any serious notions of tending a spiritual life, and Jesus Christ practically never butts in. The barriers of indifference I've stacked up are too thick."

I'd never been belligerent about deciding not to believe. I just walked away from the stress of trying to argue myself back into it. When I tried, the exercise seemed contrived. I'd bow my head and ask for guidance to believe. When the thunderbolt didn't come, I was neither surprised nor disappointed. I was never going to see it, and now it was almost imbedded in logic that I was never going to feel it, and that meant I should stop the struggle. I could still cling, I suppose, to the might-be of a life beyond this. It was a hedge.

Some blueprint for the Christian soldier!

I lit a cigarette on the train and vented a sigh. All those saints and Moses hauling his slabs down the mountain and Gabriel's horn had been pretty much blown away once I'd reached adulthood and made discoveries, fresh realities: manhood, soldiering, discovering women, beers at the German *gasthauses*, a newspaper job to go back to in the States. How much room is there on the plate?

The reason the corporal happened to come to Rome on a one-week leave from the Army camp had nothing to do with tourism or joining the herd to witness a spectacle. He was there because he didn't have the guts to admit that worship and being a card-carrying believer didn't matter any more. His mother would have died if she were to know it. So he hung onto the ornaments of his religion as a surrogate of belief. He remembered the sight of gold chalices being upraised in the solemnity of the mass in his church on the Iron Range, coming back to him like Marley's ghost in his young adulthood because by then God was a missing person in his life. No all-points bulletin to find God hit the air from the restless brain of the young man of action. God was a whiff of remembered incense. But the young soldier could see the pope. That helped him make peace with his conscience.

And why am I talking in the third person?

Maybe because it's less embarrassing that way. It's embarrassing in hindsight to remember that scene at Castel Gandolfo and to feel once more the surge of belonging that I experienced—how important that was—and at the same time realizing how barren it was of any real spiritual meaning. But the sight of that frail and smiling old man, Pius XII, the most visible living icon of the historical church, made the connection again with the church of my childhood, forcing its way into the resisting force of skepticism and just plain, dull drift. The ritual and pageantry and tradition that defined worship and God when I grew up kept reverting me, bringing me back with a stubborn power and judgmental grip. As I grew older, I felt it in a hundred different ways. I felt it in the guilt of surrendering those ornaments but also in the genuine beauty I heard and felt in that ancient liturgy: *Kyrie eleison, Christe eleison, Kyrie eleison.* It was something to hang onto when the drift I couldn't seem to reverse felt especially disturbing. So I'd return to those forms and ceremonies like a politician acting out the guidelines of the party platform.

Feeling the skin prickle when the chanting rose at Castel Gandolfo kept me in the community, at least as a formality. It was a cushion against the backslide from belief. If you want a euphemism, call it a withdrawal instead of a backslide. It made me fret now and then, but hardly gave me any round-the-clock willies. Life in that stage of my life was essentially forever. Getting close to God, finding solace in prayer, needing prayer didn't put the brakes on the lives of most of the twenty-two-year-olds I knew then, or now. So I belonged to that vast constituency of the baptized and confirmed Christians who airily ducked God but declined to surrender the perks—which were those moments of solemnity that were available if you stayed familiar with the furniture of the church, the stained glass, the hymns, the statuary, and the artifacts of its beginnings.

A few days after Castel Gandolfo I walked down into the catacombs on a rainy Saturday outside Rome near the old Appian Way. A young Italian priest was the tour guide. I was his sole client. From the chapel where I met him, we walked in the drizzle to the entrance of the catacombs. Years later I experienced Jerusalem, Bethlehem, and the Way of the Cross, and they stirred me. But this was my first connection with the actual beginnings of Christianity, and before it was over, I felt humbled and moved with a power I had not expected. I began the walk as an interested witness, far more a sightseer than a pilgrim, half-convinced I was going to see the catacombs as some reconstructed stage setting of an old Victor Mature movie. I expected the stark antiquity of it to be fascinating. This was a historic place, after all. But I had no special enthusiasm for the forthcoming narrative, the droning resanctification of the dead saints.

Will you excuse that arrogance? If not, perhaps you will forgive it.

Water dripped from some of the creases in the cavern. Some of it had been electrified, as I remember, but the priest carried a flashlight. It probed the gray-red walls and ceiling. They were mute but seemed in every deepening twist of the tunnel, with its alcoves and crudely hewn subpassages, to want to tell a story.

The narrator was not the automaton I was expecting. He gave me the history with a dignity and reverence that was almost painful. He recited the names of the martyrs interred here and he translated some of the agony and the faith of men and women facing imminent death. That torment and faith were literally written on the walls, in their own hands.

The young priest spoke sparingly, as though not wanting to molest the profundity of the sacrifice we were visiting. After a while, his reverence, the ghosts, the solemnity began to dissolve the detachment of his gourd-headed client. How could you not be enveloped by the dank intimacy of these ancient tunnels, in whose walls lay the bones of the first Christians, people willing to die in the name of their belief?

Our footfalls sent echoes through the tunnels. In some unaccountable way they seemed to connect the living and the dead 2,000 years apart. Let it happen, I told myself. You want to make the connection. You're still in the church. You belong. This is a time to genuflect.

I genuflected.

So now this connection in the Roman catacombs and events of the previous days expanded the second thoughts of the muddle-minded young Christian. Nominal Christian. Eclectic Christian. Whatever seems right. First there was the pale old hierarch speaking in a dozen tongues from a balcony in the Alban Hills, the Holy Father of my childhood. And now here were the bones and ghosts of men, women, and children who 2,000 years ago were so filled with the passion of their belief that they would flee underground like moles and die in physical misery, undefeatable.

I emerged from those tunnels with a self-serving pride in still belonging to that historic community. I belonged.

Nobody ever threw me out. Outside Castel Gandolfo I even bought a doll of the Swiss Guards who protected the Pope. One more ornament.

But I had no serious thoughts about God or faith. The props of the church were enough to carry me through the charade. Recalling this years later to a clergyman of the streets, I received an impatient huff and practically no consolation.

He asked: "What makes you think you were any different from ten million or twenty million other people your age, or any more two-faced about it? God doesn't win many popularity contests with people when they hit twenty and start finding the world. What you probably never stopped to consider was that God spent a helluva lot more energy trying to find you than the other way around."

The reverend was so forceful and annoyed that I had to smother a laugh. It must be a deflating life being God.

Does God ever work in the shadows, looking for cracks of light inviting him into the lives of restless young men and women breathing hard to build status and to start climbing the staircase? I don't know. God never confided that to me. I don't know that I gave him much of an opening. In my two years in the army, and after that building a reputation in the newspaper business, getting married, building a house and having two children, what we now preciously call "getting in touch with our spirituality" was a no-show in my life. I didn't scoff at it. I rarely thought about it once removed from my periodic visits to the religion's furniture. I did struggle through the mandatory counseling session with a priest before my marriage in 1954, and I did show up in a confession box at the Minneapolis Basilica three days before our wedding. It was part of the ritual of belonging, the membership dues, and I curdled at the thought of doing anything at that stage that would get me evicted from the club. In the confessional I hedged on my worst transgressions and ignored others. The priest was invisible. All those solemn murmurings between us were sealed and inviolate. I knew that. The knowledge wasn't persuasive enough to make me honest. A confession before priest and God is a travesty unless it is full and it is clothed in contrition. I dogged it. I'd reduced the solemnity of this act, and the prostration before God that it assumed, to a bureaucratic form that had to be observed to keep me respectable in the eyes of the wardens of the church.

In retrospect, it was pretty craven conduct. Who was I duping? The priest? God? Neither, very likely. In the confessional I was running a scam, filling the dual role of perpetrator and victim. The hypocrisy got worse and vaguely comical. Rose and I were married in the sacristy of a church at Marquette University in Milwaukee, where her Swiss-born parents lived. The locale met one more of the legal requirements, to be married in a Catholic setting. Rose was Protestant, although not combatively so. She had no objection to the sacristy. Beside this, the sacristy was a calmer venue than any other we could afford. It seemed to embrace our partnership ecumenically. She'd agreed to raise the children as Catholics. But I didn't insist, and they weren't, which meant that my wife spent many more fruitful Sunday mornings attending her church than I spent not attending mine.

Remembering those times, I can't truthfully say today that I was much hounded by remorse for having abandoned God.

Abandoned God.

How is that for spacey logic? As though God were on probation and missed the cut.

On days when I attended services, I'd privately do a critique of the minister's rhetoric and his skills at projection rather than exploring his message. I'd study the advancing queues of parishioners heading for the Communion rail, their heads lowered and lips moving. I looked on them with envy. There was something in their lives that mattered beyond the hassles and prizes of today. It showed on their faces, which seemed to declare trust and humility. On some days, I'd tell myself, "That's a beautiful thing. Why can't I have it or feel it?"

There was no reason why not. I didn't have it or feel it because it wasn't important enough. The me in my life was more important. The urgency of that was too entrenched for me to consider simple humility, and to try to distinguish between reality (what I did every day) and life (the beauty of a spiritual commitment that I avoided with my self-indulgence).

Still, I felt goaded to look for God. Some of the myths of religion, I'd tell myself, obscured the view and warred with the intellect. A lot of the biblical lore looked and sounded invented, which made it a handy excuse to dodge God. It felt comfortable to consign God to the dark holes of mystery in a universe that as I child I was convinced was the creation of God. But now the logicians pretty much agreed that it banged itself into existence, which put God in some kind of scientific limbo. It made God more nebulous than ever. Every periodical in the country had some kind of cover story asking if God is dead. Despite my own spins on the subject, that kind of speculation offended me. I wanted somehow to defend God. So, I said, all right, let God equal x . Call God a mystery, but don't make him extinct. I didn't try to understand why this was bothering me so much and why I was twisting the language to keep the idea of God in my life without committing myself to belief. It was a pretty ungainly piece of somersaulting, and I can suspect now that somebody, maybe God, was conducting a guerrilla action to keep me in the game. How do I know that? Who finds whom in this chase? Where do we, for example, find God? For a while, in my young married life, I thought I looked everywhere—the church, the heavens, the Sunday missal, the votive candles. I didn't look very energetically, but I cased practically the whole landscape. One place I didn't search was in my own heart.

I looked for spirituality in other places. I thought I found it in the high country, with all of the symbolism that went with mountain tops and glorious sunsets.

That was a masquerade. But I half-believed it, and I preached it for years before discovering that God doesn't give gold stars, or necessarily peace, on the summits of mountains.

3

Riding an Express Lane to Nowhere

When I visited the doctor's office in the 1960s and 1970s, I scurried through the medical history part of the paperwork before a physical exam and put the routine "x" in the "no" column. No diabetes, strokes, or major surgery. No gout or trench mouth.

Here was a line reading "alcoholism?"

Well, what about it? Alcoholism is finding yourself in Newark when you meant to fly to Atlanta. Alcoholism is falling off the barstool or urinating into the kitchen sink. I checked "no" without pause. Everyone ties one on a few times a year.

An hour later the doctor would confirm my personal diagnosis. I was healthy. I was also on the move, a newspaperman traveling first with the Minnesota Vikings professional football team and later with politicians like Hubert Humphrey and Eugene McCarthy and the whole spectrum of fascinating characters who populate the journalist's world. At night I'd come home to the tidy chalet Rose and I built in the then-pastoral suburb of Plymouth west of Minneapolis. Our two daughters, Amy and Meagan, attended school in the prosperous neighboring suburb of Wayzata. I was an accredited member of the American Legion and a part-time shortstop on the neighborhood softball team. What more marvels did life hold? The day wasn't long enough. I was sizzling with

34

energy, and I aired it out in a dozen directions. I wrote daily for the Minneapolis newspaper, first on pro football and then as an opinion columnist, gave speeches, conducted a radio talk show and a TV public affairs show, began writing books, raised money for the disadvantaged, biked long distances in the summer, skied and camped in snow caves in the winter, organized adventure travel for hundreds of outdoor activists in a club I formed, leaped out of airplanes by parachute, and wedged in a week or two in that chaos of action to climb mountains—the Matterhorn, the Grand Tetons, Mount Rainier, the Matterhorn, in the Himalayas and the Andes, the Matterhorn. The Matterhorn was hypnotic for me. I kept returning. Avidly.

Compulsively.

And in all of this speedorama of life, I still found myself looking for some kind of repose, something to redeem all of that velocity.

I needed more than peace. I needed a sedative and at least a year's sabbatical on a bleak island someplace in the Bering Straits to consider the potential lunacy of all this. But ignoring hindsight, I can't say I considered it lunacy at the time. I put a different spin on it. This was maximizing my vitalities and my urges. It was grabbing time by the neck and shaking it out so that it was lean and usable at 5 A.M. or at 10 P.M. It was making money, creating the persona of some all-purpose, round-the-clock troubadour and Jack Armstrong, staying a step ahead of folk who didn't harbor all those urges. It was a schedule that burlesqued the instructions of old Rudyard Kipling, filling each unforgiving minute with something as long as it wasn't calm and quiet.

And in six or seven years of this, my life approached midpoint. The graph showed this: I was entering thousands of homes every day as a columnist, making a difference on some of those days, running on a half-dozen tracks professionally. But spiritually—insofar as it entered my mind—I was essentially a mess. I don't want to pound on myself excessively. Say I was looking. For what? Fame? No, not that. I was drawn to excitement. Sometimes to risk. I needed the feeling of relevance, whether it was writing a newspaper column that changed minds today, or solving a reader's problem privately with a phone call to the bureaucracy. Newspapering, risk on a mountain, gabbing with listeners on a talk show were fulfilling in ways that evaded easy definition. Maybe a word might help: involvement. So the résumé went: professionally a columnist-town crier visible and serviceably respected in the city where I worked, a teller of stories and a singer of songs, a public conscience and a prosecutor of the exploiters and the connivers. I became a juggler of my crisscrossing careers and passions. Daily and almost hourly I felt the gratification of what seemed upfront to be a useful life. I could find housing for a homeless family through the newspaper. Some days I could express what was in the heart of the reader. I could stand on the summit of the Matterhorn and suck in the cold west wind and feel almost invincible. It wasn't braggadocio. I'd earned this and treasured it.

And then I remembered the lyrics of Peggy Lee's song: "Is that all there is?"

God, there must be more.

The adventurer in me had energy but no special vision. There was more, but my agendas obscured what I couldn't see happening in my own house. At work I could entertain or build an awareness of an injustice or in a speech create a consensus in the audience. I might be able to lead it to understand the casual cruelties we as a society inflict on people who are voiceless or different. But the excitement of it blinded me to the neglect I was inflicting on my wife, my children, my marriage, and on what should have been the governing values in my own life—values that had to do with love and care-giving and brotherhood. I did feel needles of conscience about that. A person, after all, wants to be whole. He can't very well be whole without sensibility. He can't be whole riding a high-speed carousel every day of the year. I credited myself with sensibility. When I had time, I gave love and care, felt good about it, and then shifted into the faster track, putting love and care on hold.

I don't think this made me an impostor. It made me self-centered. It made me care liberally for my ego. I measured my worth not by the comfort and support I could bring into the lives of those nearest me, or into the lives of strangers for that matter, but by the raw production I poured into the day with whatever creativity was within me. One of my codes was borrowed from an old axiom of the corporate executive: If you want a job done, give it to somebody who's busy. I was busy. If my work load for the day was choked, I could pack in one more newspaper story, a drive to St. Paul to give a lift to a colleague stranded by car trouble. I stretched out the day. Maybe I was postponing the drive home, wary about arriving there in time to be a chummy father who had to be full of happy nods of approval scanning the test papers.

God, was it that bad?

I think it was. I'd make one more telephone call before leaving the office, two more or three, and then call home. And, of course, there was still time to stop for a drink. Get home at 7:30. Groggy. Five minutes of conversation with my wife. I don't remember asking often how things went during the day for her at the elementary school where she taught. She often asked what I'd written for tomorrow. I identified the subject, but our minds rarely came together with any serious attempt at intimacy in act or thought on my part. There was time for a hug for the kids, although maybe not. I was in bed before 9:30 P.M., half-exhausted.

Have you heard this before? Probably. It may summarize a part of your own life. Where was the reward in a day like that? The satisfaction was in getting all of it done with some reasonable coherence and skill, which meant pride: pride in meeting deadlines, both the occupational ones and the artificial ones created by a self-designated dynamo, pride in managing the chaos.

Some murmurings from my insides told me there was a more generous way to live, but I held onto that madcap pace for years because—although I kept denying this—it became my identity.

Into this, increasingly, I stirred booze.

Not much at home. And I rarely went off on arm-flailing drunks. I kept it away from my work insofar as I could. I usually drank alone, often when no one was . . . was what?

Was watching. Worried in the early 1970s, I joined an Alcoholics Anonymous group. I went without liquor for five years. But I never made the first admission—that I couldn't handle it.

A respected Minnesota poet who was dogged much of his life by alcoholism—the disease that eventually killed him—put together a film offering an alternative to the exhilaration generated by booze. He wrote the script during one of his attempts at recovery. I'd met him. He was a marvelous writer. I saw the film during one of my own attempts at recovery. The ideas in it were uncannily familiar. In fact, in some of my presumptuous hours in midlife when I believed I'd freed myself from the seductive psychosis of drinking-for-a-high, I preached some of those ideas as a visiting speaker at A.A. meetings.

"If we need a psychological fix in our lives, an extended high," I said, "the road for us is to find one that's safe, one that keeps us away from the artificial and destructive high of chemicals." The poet's film offered a variety of options to chemicals as a source for this kind of boost. Music was one. A strong relationship of mutual trust was another. A healthy physical act or feat, good for body and mind, and even for the soul, was another.

In other words, a mountaintop experience could do it, reaching the summit after a tough climb, a commitment fulfilled.

With this notion the poet's words drifted out of his world of metaphors into my own world of edging up cliffs to stand in the wind and sun on the top of the mountain. For years I'd really believed a mountain climb could produce the euphoria to expel the demons that kept me going back to the bottle. It's not why I climbed. But in later years I deluded myself into believing that the gratification of a successful climb was some sort of craggy therapy session that made me less alcoholic.

It didn't. I don't want to minimize the importance of finding options to the airy effects of drinking. But for me the ultimate lesson came as clear as a quart of vodka, and it was one in which the poet might have concurred if he lived long enough: Recovery from alcoholism takes something deeper than the creation of a surrogate for the bottle.

I'm writing now through the filter of years of nursing those illusions, beginning relatively early in my life. I'm also sighing in some incredulity, realizing that in the midst of the oncoming alcoholism and my easy denials of it, I was actually trying to concoct some peace of mind.

I didn't pray for that peace. I didn't ask God or his lieutenants to help me find a way to discover God's will for me. I was then an entrenched materialist, and I had no confidence that any prayers from me were going to get a sympathetic hearing.

That is a pretty dismal skewing of theology, I know now.

But theology did not command prime-time billing in my life then, and God was indistinguishable from the iconography of stained glass and haloed statues. Was God actually somebody, something? Was there someone, a divinity, so powerful and engulfing that it directed the universe, directed our lives, and did it with a love both universal and personal? And because of our gratitude for this bounty, it, or he or she, deserved love in return?

When I thought about it, I ran into walls. It was a wonder to contemplate, but I couldn't shake the fairy tale part of it. I took consolation. There had to be millions of people like me, wanting to be in that place of belief, but not being able to seriously grasp it. God was still clouds and never-never land.

In later years, trying to find the more generous way, I read Thomas Merton, the late Catholic monk, writer-poet, and wise man. One of his books he called *No Man Is an Island*, borrowing the concept of John Donne, the recognition that none of us lives in isolation. Our lives our interconnected in enduring ways, and we depend on each other. Thomas

Merton's words telescoped the life I'd been living and the futility of my random search for a personal peace while I was devouring time with my prodigal energy.

"We do not live merely in order to 'do something'—no matter what," Merton wrote:

> Activity is just one of the normal expressions of life, and the life it expresses is all the more perfect when it sustains itself with an ordered economy of action. This order demands a wise alternation of activity and rest. We do not live more fully merely by doing more, seeing more, tasting more, and experiencing more than we ever have before. On the contrary, some of us need to discover that we will not begin to live more fully until we have the courage to do and see and taste and experience much less than usual.
>
> A tourist may go through a museum with a Baedeker, looking conscientiously at everything important, and come out less alive than when he went in. He has looked at everything and seen nothing. . . .
>
> There are times, then, when in order to keep ourselves in existence at all we simply have to sit back for a while and do nothing. And for a man who has let himself be drawn completely out of himself by his activity, nothing is more difficult than to sit still and rest, doing nothing at all. The very act of resting is the hardest and most courageous act he can perform: and often it is quite beyond his power.

How much had I been trying to taste, Thomas Merton? The whole twelve courses of experience piled onto the plate, everyday, whether trifling or important. I'd arrive at the sound of the bell each day with this gargantuan platter, poised at the head of what the Scandinavians call a smorgasbord.

And why couldn't I see that my obsession with doing was chewing me up systematically, feeding my pride by loading something, anything, into those unforgiving minutes and days? Again, Merton wrote:

The value of our activity depends almost entirely on the humility to accept ourselves as we are. The reason why we do things so badly is that we are not content to do what we can.

We insist on doing what is not asked of us, because we want to taste the success that belongs to somebody else.

We never discover what it is like to make a success of our own work, because we do not want to undertake any work that is merely proportionate to our powers.

Who is willing to be satisfied with a job that expresses all his limitations?

So don't express those limitations. Overpower them. I may not be the best bungee jumper. I may even harbor some contempt for bungee jumping as a recreation. But I did bungee jump. I may have been afraid to climb the Devil's Tower, but I did climb it. Why? Override fear. Pack in the minutes. Stretch the limits. If kayaking or horseback riding or being alone scare you at all, do it or find it. Get better at it. Chase some of the other phantoms of your life. Exorcise them. Plow into the challenges.

Like who? Well, maybe Don Quixote. But you may recognize something here in your own life. It may say much about the human condition of the twentieth century. It doesn't say much about humility. I'll allow this: I wasn't so compulsive about finding gratification and strokes for my exertions that I ignored the traps. In the times when I'd apologize for the selfishness of this kind of living, to my wife or to myself, I could see and feel the void in my life.

I could see and feel it when I looked into the eyes of a woman who'd just lost her teenage son in a car crash. She was trying to be responsive to the inquiring journalist, trying to be courteous in the terrible fog of her grief. She mourned the loss of one she'd loved above anyone else on earth. "What I remember best about him," she said, "were the goofy things he said out of the blue when he came rushing into the kitchen from school. He used the language teenagers do and I didn't have the faintest idea what he was talking about, and he'd see that I was bewildered by all of it and then he would grab me and hug me and say, "Mom, you're the coolest. The greatest."

She spoke with such utter dignity, with such acceptance of her son's death as the will of someone beyond her, that I couldn't stop my tears. This was her spiritual strength and her gift. There was something touching her at this very moment. I wouldn't have called it God's grace then. I think I would now. It made her whole.

I didn't have her peace. At those and other hours, I sought it. Maybe, I can say now, this was a beginning. But if the goal was discovery, it was a beginning I laced with easy and self-defeating shortcuts. I was looking for simple truth. What made it so hard for me to accept what the woman felt so modestly but so unshakably? What made it so hard was the pretense. I pretended devotion. I connected the moments of tranquillity and awe I felt in the outdoors with the presence of God. God may very well have been present in those moments. Who's going to keep him out? But it was a facile and sneaky way to contrive a spiritual feeling that didn't come naturally. It was like the person you'll see casting beatific eyes at a painting in a gallery, staring that way for minutes on end, or least long enough for the other onlookers to get the idea that here is a person absolutely anointed by the experience, floating in a zone of inspiration.

You can pretty well tell when it's an act. And I can pretty well tell today that the union with God I pretended to feel on a mountain slope was partly a tribute to the power and beauty of the day and of nature, and partly a self-deception. I did feel the gift of the mountain solitude at sunrise. I did feel thankful for it. I would even kneel and thank God.

And I wrote then: "There are reasons why we feel healed when we return from a quiet weekend on the forest trail. We feel cleansed. We may have walked that trail alone, but we did not feel alone. Our thoughts were generous. Our workaday resentments were banked. Why did we wonder afterward what had happened to us?"

I believe now there is a grace on that forest trail if it can create such a transformation in us. But the experience is shallow, the feeling of consecration it gives us is false if we do not draw on that experience and dig deeper into why we so eagerly yield ourselves to turmoil and the gratifications of self the rest of the week, the rest of the year.

For me, the benign quality of those moments in the forest were real. I would hold my breath to try to preserve them, the serenity seemed that deep. But for me it was not a communion. It was a reprieve from the eagerness to get back into the express lane.

What was missing was simple and unequivocal faith. I knelt, but it was a gesture, a ritual. It was not a union.

What I didn't recognize was that unearthing the spiritual part of who we are may actually take some sacrifice and some contrition.

Imagine recognizing that?

I found that was much harder to do than filling those unforgiving minutes by being profound or being frantic. It wasn't as much fun, either, and it was even harder to do with a mind hazed by alcohol. The speed, the alcohol, the squandering of my energies eventually put another God into my life. Freedom. I needed freedom to explore all the potential of an expanding life.

I achieved this freedom by divorcing my wife of twenty-two years, a good woman who understood my compulsions and my selfishness, and still forgave. I removed myself from the house of my children, one fifteen years old, the other twelve.

But the God of Freedom was a slippery one. What the God of Freedom gave me was isolation in the middle of the crowd, deeper than any I'd ever felt.

4

Stumbling into Church with a Hangover

The outside steps of the church were set at a modest pitch, member-friendly. They should have been easily negotiable. But to a man entering the church on a sunless December morning with his mind sunk in remorse, they looked liked the pyramid of Cheops.

I stumbled once. It might have been excusable. I was hung over from a night of intermittent drinking. I'd slept for two hours, once somewhere before midnight, in somebody else's house, and then just before dawn after I returned to my bachelor apartment to discover I'd left the key at the other house. Remembering this, I rocked in futility on the church steps. Could there have been another night filled with so much self-abuse?

At the door of my apartment a few hours before, I'd remembered the credit card maneuver. If your hands were steady enough, you could slip a credit card between the door and the frame and trip the lock. My hands were steady enough, but my eyes had trouble lining up the crack next to the frame. I was in the process of negotiating this hurdle when another apartment dweller entered the hall, stopped and froze, convinced he had stumbled onto a break-in. I had enough self-possession to identify myself as the owner of the apartment whose lock I was trying to slip. I explained the reason for it. I offered to present my driver's license, which might have been the night's final ignominy. He nodded uncertainly but walked to his apartment and made no comment.

I was drunk and practically sleepless and breaking into my own place like a common thief. Are these the acts of a mature man nearing fifty? I opened the door and heaved myself into a chair, too bushed and inept to pull off my overcoat. Common thievery was acceptable alongside my behavior of the previous eight hours. I'd spent three or four hours in a couple of bars, called a woman friend early in the evening, had sex with her, left to have dinner in a steak house nearby, called another woman friend later in the evening, had sex with her, drank a couple of nightcaps, drove home staring into the rearview mirror for lurking squad cars, slept an hour after I got home, and woke up crying.

In the newspaper that morning, a Sunday, one of my columns was going to appear in a prominent position in the paper, accessible to hundreds of thousands of readers. It detailed a story of a mentally retarded man, struggling to achieve self-sufficiency, seeing employment doors closed to him day after day in the rounds he made to find work rather than to live on doles. A few days before, a small businessman offered him a job for $4.50 an hour, stacking reams of paper. The man who was disabled hadn't abandoned hope or his search. This was his day of victory, the day when the rest of the world finally seemed to be telling him: You belong. That may not be what the world was telling him, but it's what he heard. It was a good story, one to warm the December morning for anyone who remotely understood the retarded man's struggle, or even for those who might not. It had heroes: the man who persevered, the one who hired him. The story seemed passably well told. It spared the reader any overt sermon about a lonely and limited man dealing with life with whatever small gifts he had to give it, while millions of others among us groaned and railed about trivia. I concede that the message was somewhere between the lines if the reader thought to consider it.

When I woke up in the chair, I looked at my watch and suddenly imagined a scene. In thousands of homes in Minnesota at that very moment, newspaper readers were being introduced to a brave and disciplined man who overcame a damaged brain to achieve a goal of independence. At that moment somewhere in Minneapolis, this man must be very proud.

At the same moment, the author of this story sat in a chair in his apartment six or seven miles away, wearing the street clothes and overcoat he'd slept in, smelling of booze and sweat, trying to fight off his shame, and weeping quietly because he couldn't.

I stood and spoke a few words aloud: "You goddamned bum."

A bum because my response to a broken relationship after my divorce was alley-cat morality and a crashing end to the sobriety I'd been trying to nurse through the late forties of my life. A bum because while I understood personal discipline and facing adversity and sacrifice, and brought into the lives of newspaper readers dozens of people whose own lives shone with those qualities, I was dealing with my own emotional adversity by bombing out. I felt like a fraud.

In the shower, I slapped my face. "Get out of it," I said. "Do something. This morning you may be a bum, but you're also a human being."

I made an apology. I don't know to whom. I just said, "I'm sorry."

And then I said, "God, I don't know where to go. I need help."

Look who's asking for help. A man of action and ideas; a man of logic and verve, capable of climbing mountains, of juggling six agendas in a span of twenty-four hours, ladies and gentleman, a span of twenty-four hours.

Today, transposing myself ahead twenty years into the here and now, I can conjure the wry voice of God that morning: "I was beginning to wonder how long it would take him."

I drank two cups of coffee and drove out of the parking lot. I honestly didn't know my destination. I wanted to get out in the air and start acting normally again and, also, not so incidentally, I had to cover a pro football game at the stadium at noon. I filled up with gasoline at a service station and exchanged a few words with the attendant about Minnesota weather. Normalcy. Feeling better, I bought the Sunday morning newspaper, intending to read it over a plate of scrambled eggs at a nearby diner. More normalcy.

But I didn't. It was 8:15, just fifteen minutes before the start of worship at a Lutheran church where I'd attended services at the invitation of a friend a few months before. I knew the pastor, Arvid (Bud) Dixen, from meetings at a ministerial association where I'd spoken and from a couple columns I'd written about Bud's creative religion—a tailgate party in the church parking lot to compete with Sunday football on TV.

I also remembered a little speech I made an hour before: "God, I don't know where to go."

Someone, something gave directions.

In the narthex of the Edina Community Lutheran Church, I ran into the reverend as he was rushing to his office to answer a phone. He seemed somewhat startled. I don't think his surprise was induced by a stranger coming into his church. More likely it was my appearance that stopped him. I'd shaved but must have drooped from all masts. "Good morning," he said. "I've got this phone call. Come into the office."

The shepherds know when one of the sheep needs first aid.

He said we could talk at greater length, but for now, what could I tell him? "I need to change something," I said, "I want to."

He put an arm on my shoulder and said, "Most of us do. Come and worship with us."

His text happened to be about forgiveness, about the divine quality of it, about the hope it could give us. Nobody lived, he was saying, who was beyond God's forgiveness. His eyes looked into mine a couple of times, and he smiled ironically, because he was an ironic kind of guy in private life, a man who often spoofed the theological anguish zealously practiced by some of the Lutheran clergy. He seemed to be saying, "Well, all right, if you came here to parade your guilt and self-loathing, you probably came to the wrong door. If you came here for shelter from a bad time in your life, we can help."

How?

Why I came was not to confess. I'd already done that. My appearance, my obvious despair, was admission enough. I came because I needed faces and voices around me, declaring their needs, affirming their belief. I needed to belong to something where there was hope and acceptance. The surface fulfillments in my life, the work and deeds and the visibility I got for them, weren't enough to preserve the self-respect that had been eroding for years and which, on the morning after this ugly night, had fallen into the sewer.

A beginning for me was to get back into a church.

But organized religion—I'd heard it a hundred times—isn't the same as spirituality.

I'd heard it from speakers at my earlier A.A. meetings, from reformed hippies who'd gone to Kathmandu to experience conversion in the Himalayas, from friends who were convinced their lives had been distorted by church dogma or who'd been bored by mediocrity in the pulpit, and I'd heard it from ministers themselves.

The failures of organized Christianity have been, to be charitable about it, colossal when they're arrayed against the simple but hard tenets of Christianity as spoken by the man in whose name the movement began. You can begin with the mass murder and medieval corruptions inflicted by its hierarchs and its self-designated avengers. A vice just as grievous in the minds of some of its sterner critics in the ministry is organized religion's determined retreat from the footsteps of Jesus Christ in how it acts as a social conscience. And there is the dismal spectacle of the institution of the church being captured by dictators, parliaments, political revolutions, military adventurers, and possibly by television. Those takeovers are well documented. So is the abdication by some churches of the Christian charter to be a sanctuary for sinners and misfits, the oddballs of society, and a fountainhead for hope for those misfits.

There are voices of conscience in many of the churches of today. They will bring up the picture of Jesus Christ dining with sinners, telling us that before we can save our lives we have to lose them, telling us to give it all away, living and preaching as a social radical. And then the voices of conscience will draw another picture—of thousands of mainstream churches in America today playing it safe, the shepherds worried about offending the congregation, worried about their churches being too cordial in welcoming gays, lesbians, and social outcasts, about churches acting in a de facto way as the adjutants for the consensus political attitudes of the time.

Clearly there are brave people in the pulpit who won't let their congregations forget what the man in the sandals said. They also won't let them forget what he meant. But when we look at churches today, we have a clashing composite—of the language that churches quote from the Bible being contradicted by the failure of many of them to act on that language and its convictions.

I suppose I understood all of that when I walked into the church on the December morning. I imposed no integrity test on this church that morning, although that particular church might have scored better than most. I didn't walk into the church to evaluate it. I came because I felt inhuman. I came to be healed and to be accepted. The start for me was to hear the language again, from those fearsome pronouncements in the Old Testament to those parables of the man in sandals. They were the stories that often sounded elliptical when I first heard them. By and large, many of them still sound that way after I've listened to three generations of preachers and seminary gurus fumbling to interpret the message without sounding hopelessly obsolete or condescending.

Not long after I walked into that church, I went to the mat with the other voice in me. It asked: *The man in the sandals, Jesus of Nazareth. Was this guy for real? Who was he?*

I don't know. The Scripture insists that he was the Son of Man, the Son of God, Redeemer, Counselor. George Handel says the same thing in a chorus of four hundred voices.

Do you believe it? The other voice was asking.

I try.

If you worship in a Christian church and believe in God, can you still call yourself a Christian without truly accepting the divinity of Christ, free of doubt?

Anybody can worship in a Christian church. I've seen murderers, all but convicted, worshiping in a Christian church. Thieves, whores, embezzlers, and outrageous con men, none of whom may have told the truth in ten years and have no thought of reforming, can worship in a Christian church. People who have lost their self-respect to alcohol can worship in a Christian church.

That's an ambiguous answer.

It may be. But I think Jesus Christ would have given it.

The other voice again: *If this is so much of a muddle to you, why do you pray to him today?*

It helps. It comforts me. I feel closer to understanding.

But you didn't that Sunday morning when you went back to a church in desperation.

I went back because, for me, there were no other roads. My other voice suddenly took a vow of silence. The other voice, if you'll pardon the caveat, wasn't my licensed devil's advocate. The voice asked questions that were legitimate for me and that I'd asked myself a hundred times. But there were no other roads for me. I went into the church because for all of its institutional warts, I had respect for it, and it was the only place I could think of where I could begin to be cleansed.

It didn't matter how many times I've listened to a bumbling preacher or tried to outlast a windy one or tried to fathom a brilliant one. It didn't matter how many magazine articles I'd read about church congregations going for glitz, enshrining prosperity, or others going yahoo over guitar-plucking concerts and calling this worship; or other congregations splitting over abortion or homosexuality; and others ready to haul out court injunctions and razor blades in an intramural fight over giving a home to illegal aliens.

Most of this congregational groin-kicking concludes when all combatants lower their heads and make the prayerful avowal that the preceding bloodletting was all done for the sake of Jesus Christ, Son of God and our Lord.

For all of the historic and cultural scabs it carries, the church, that particular church because it was close at hand, was a haven for me. Somebody else might have chosen a psychologist, or mother, or called in to a talk show. Maybe 911. I'm not saying it wouldn't have been right for that person or even that it wouldn't have been more productive, if you need instant results to tend to your mortification. The church was my place because there were people in it. There was a community in it. I'm ready to agree that the word *community* has been drenched with overuse and imagery to the point where it is almost impossible to look at any assembly of like-minding people, from a reunion of sandpaper salesmen to an arena full of basketball fanatics, without somebody calling it a "community."

But a church truly is, or must be, community in the most solemn and uplifting sense. It is an invitation to sit with, kneel with, sing with, suffer with, and worship with those who seek what you do, the humility to serve and the strength to understand.

I'll admit to being less rigorous than some others who debate "spirituality vs. organized religion." I find myself less harsh than some of my friends in judging "church." All right, as an institution it's been a wall-to-wall historical mess. But looking into those impassive faces around me on Sunday mornings, I tell myself that the most strident critics must be short-changing the value of church in our society and in our world. Let's say you discount as a delusion the ideas that it brings spiritual comfort and healing into the lives of those who worship there, which is a pretty arrogant leap for any critic to make. What you should not discount, simply as a citizen, is the willingness you see in those often-scorned hymn singers to respond to hunger and grief and the rest of the catalog of human need. In other words, church as a food shelf for millions, as a refuge of hope for the homeless. This is what it can be, and if it has to be defended, that might be defense enough.

When I look at church in its most benign light, as a servant, I don't want to overlook the perversions of organized religion and the comical infighting. But I also look at it as a house for giving, which is an act fundamental to our humanity. I look at it sometimes as a journalist, as a person who has recorded government's systematic retreat from giving, and also recorded the sickeningly deep gulf between those who are comfortable and secure in our society and those who have little or nothing and practically no prospect of changing that. I look at the giving I see in churches as one who has traveled in Africa and Asia and South America and witnessed starvation.

And then I picture the dozens of scenes of men and women, mostly women, dragging their grocery bags into church in the dead of winter, and multiplying that by thousands and thousands, and then by more thousands to build classrooms in Tanzania and Uganda and Madagascar. They are lands where I have seen the native kids weeping in the grips of their emotions when, for the first day, they could read their books and write their lessons under a roof, instead of doing it under an equatorial sun or under rocks. The money to build that roof came from a church.

But wait a minute. The other voice is butting in again. *Aren't most churches speckled with hypocrites, Sunday morning grandstanders, people giving themselves a pretext to look and sound devout, hymn-singing robots who have figured out a way to dodge the hard questions about faith and commitment and trust?*

Yeah, they are.

Do you meet all or part of that description?

Part of it, yes.

Aren't you deceiving yourself, then, postponing a true spiritual experience you might not be capable of achieving, by showing up every Sunday morning in your tie and sweater, with something for the basket, a quavering tenor for the opening hymn? Aren't you deceiving yourself by swapping "God be with you"s around the pews at greeting time and finishing up the devotional with a cup of coffee and a caramel roll? Is that how we become spiritual?

It's probably better than ninety-six hours of discover-yourself therapy and trying to find God in a mayflower.

I wasn't really ignoring a spiritual experience, I thought.

On that December Sunday I was trying to draw from the generosity of strangers, needing their embrace of acceptance. I needed to bow my head at the time of Communion and to hear from the server, "This is the body of Christ, given for you."

And then I felt, for a moment, at least, the precious gift of reconciliation.

If I didn't understand, even if I didn't believe, I felt the forgiveness of somebody, something. On my way back to the pew, I found myself defining what it was I'd been missing. The things that were wrong with my behavior—a divorce, drinking, idealizing "competence" at work. Production and achievement to the neglect of my relationships. Dodging codes of personal morality. These had ripped the center out of my life. I couldn't honestly call family my center any more, nor work. I hadn't gone so far as to elevate material success that high.

Getting back to church was the rediscovery of a center. It was a reunion with the idea of searching and being cleansed. But if it was a reunion, why not with the big church of my childhood? The church with its remembered incense, the grins and frights from my catechism classes, the massive impregnability and immortality of it that I felt when I stood before the Basilica of Saint Peter in Rome.

In my depression of the Sunday morning in December, I drove to the Lutheran church whose pastor I knew. I did it because of simple church scenes I recalled. My recollections may not have been fair. Most of my experience in the Catholic church was connected with my boyhood and adolescence. I attended first because the family required it. The First Communion and confirmation were mandatory. Burning in hell for an indeterminate term was the probable option. But when I remember Father Mike's brazen coaching at the confirmation scene—that silent outburst of "you dummy" and all—I grant that it wasn't great theology, but it was hard to ignore, and I treasure the scene.

So it's hard to deny the affection those memories had created for me as part of my days of worship in the Catholic church. As a young adult and student I discovered soon enough why it was no longer *the* church of Christianity, why Martin Luther and Calvin and the others rebelled, and, later, why its preachments on social issues, its monolithic structure and the institution of the papacy in Rome have attracted the hostility and the revulsion of millions through the centuries. Much of this, I'm sure, was earned. Part of it is now outdated.

I'm sure you harbor only limited interest in one man's transition from the Catholic to the Lutheran church for his Sunday morning services. But since my later spiritual struggle—perhaps like yours—carried such intimate echoes of the religion of my childhood, I thought the reader deserves an accounting. I've never considered it a rebellion. In my maturing years when I formed social attitudes, I concluded this: the Catholic church's rigid attitudes on birth control, the refusal of the Vatican to allow women into the priesthood, and its refusal to allow priests to marry in today's world is a loyalty to the Stone Age that is both inexcusable and destructive to the church. And yet in casual arguments about religion with some of my friends (a few of whom inevitably become former friends) I defend much of what the Catholic church has done in this century. I bring up some of its leadership in uplifting the minorities in America when it wasn't very popular, the progressive and sometimes courageous political attitudes of its organization of American bishops today, and some of its works in South America and Africa. What I do mostly is remember it sentimentally from my days as a boy. It follows that you're are not going to hear from me some of today's orthodox indictments by former Catholics who blame the church for wrecking their lives, when a substantial part of the damage was done by the plaintiffs themselves.

But on the day when I needed to be folded into the arms of a forgiving family of worshipers, to regain part of the humanity I'd lost, I didn't return to the church of my childhood. I can't honestly tell you that this act grew out of a conviction that Norwegian Lutherans in Minnesota practice forgiveness more fervidly than Irish (or German or Slovenian) Catholics and have acquired that trait through long exposure to rhetorical abuse from Swedes. What I'd missed in the years when I slid away from practicing the faith was the realization that Catholic church congregations are just as sociable today and, all right, as aware of church as community, as Norwegian Lutherans and English Episcopalians. If the truth were known, they may be more so. But when I was a kid, I didn't see the communal horseplay at the church dinners, I didn't know about potlucks, or the support the congregation gave to those mourning the death of loved ones.

I didn't know, in other words, about my old church's compassions. But in my later years I'd seen care, something close to family, on the faces of people mingling after the service at churches like the one where the pastor I knew preached.

So I went to this church.

I will begin to try to find God, I said, at the beginning. I don't think I meant finding God. I meant finding myself or finding, as I have said in another time, my soul. If I could manage that, sooner or later I would overtake God—who, of course, was not fleeing at all. I was doing all of the running, running on the treadmill. So returning to church in a serious way gave me hope. But I learned early in this new adventure that looking to the generosity of others, rejoining the family, was probably looking into the wrong place for the ultimate answer. The place to find that was in my own head and soul.

5

An Empty Prayer

Two years after I began worshiping as a Lutheran the new pastor of our church invited me to join three other members of the congregation in speaking at an informal program the evening before Thanksgiving Day. The pastor was Mark Hanson, later a bishop, a man who has never been terrified by the idea of experimentation. I wasn't designated as the congregational strange fish on the program, but that probably was the idea. My early history in the Catholic church and my relative newness to the group may have constituted my chief credentials to look at this Lutheran congregation. I acknowledged my Roman roots and expressed hope that the alien cast of my Slavic hair wouldn't arouse undo suspicion among the torsk-loving Norwegians in our group.

They smiled carefully in the Norwegian Lutheran style. I thanked them for their leap of faith in welcoming me into their number. In due time I offered a more serious kind of thanks in this week of thanksgiving, to God, for the gift of the Eucharist. And I then raised a question: Why was it, I asked, that so many Protestant churches had trouble installing Communion as a weekly centerpiece of worship?

I had some hesitation about bringing it up. Maybe not here and now, I thought. Maybe this was a scene of a child of the Eucharist-conscious Catholic church exacting some mischievous revenge on the Bible-toting Protestants. I suspected that most of them agreed on the value of receiving of

Communion more often. Yet, I don't really know how they interpreted my small testimony. I still don't. What do I know about Swedes and Norwegians behind those buttermilk eyebrows and their historic civility? What I do know now is that the reverend himself shared my view of the virtues of weekly Communion, and so did other Lutheran churches. And it was a movement clearly in progress and had nothing to do with my thoughts, unblushingly Catholic as they were.

I'd become a weekly churchgoer. This, I said, is a better path. I can do my internal wrestlings about God while I'm listening to Gospels and sermons, threading through lessons and the singing of Psalms. Listening to the sermons exhumed the paradoxes of religion and worship that have always fascinated me. Often, sitting in the pew, I found myself witnessing some very strenuous rhetorical gymnastics in the pulpit. I did it with some sympathy and respect. It's a different world today from the one in which Jesus Christ preached. Here, for example, is a Sunday morning sermon on divorce. The ministers can't relish tackling that one. How can they? Most churches now accept divorce, conforming with the values of the society in which they serve. A case can be made, society says, for ending a marriage. Most churches concur. A destructive marriage can injure the children, to say nothing of the spouses. There can be, in other words, a humane, a logical reason for divorce. But that is not at all what the man in the sandals seemed to be saying 2,000 years ago. So when it's convenient does the church ignore his teaching, as I had done in my divorce? And if so, what does the church believe?

How is it telling us to behave?

Mixed messages like that, compounded by the inevitable politics within churches, have convinced thousands of people who look for God—who try to find "spirituality"—that the church is probably an impediment to that search. I thought about this proposition in the midst of my grapplings. I decided that I'm probably a willing captive of tradition. Church seems OK to me. If you take church seriously, I thought—and I don't know a whole lot of Lutherans who don't—you just might upgrade your behavior. You might bring some order out of the tumults in your life, reduce some of the "me" in it and find yourself closer to God.

Because I traveled, I slowly got acquainted with the culture of the Lutherans' country churches. The rural folk worshiped in those lovely old chapels with the white-frame walls and high, dignified steeples, whose bells rang out over the cornfields so evocatively. I came to love the sight of those country chapels, Lutheran or otherwise. I also got familiar with some delightful customs, the potlucks, the hospitality to strangers, and a few odd kinks of language. At one post-worship serving, the pastor confided, the chairperson of the meal had set out the coffee pots with notes in front of each, identifying one as "regular" and the other as "de-calf."

In time I felt properly institutionalized. As a relative newcomer, I avoided most of the congregational meetings. I didn't have enough time-in-grade to wrangle over mission statements, arguments that seemed to appeal to the peculiarly Lutheran instinct for congregational angst.

Not because it seemed the churchy thing to do, but because communal worship eventually demands sensible teamwork and a sincere effort at service, I got involved—and gladly. I hauled my bags of pasta cans and bags of rice on first Sunday for the food shelf, took my turn in the rotations of lectors who read the lessons, and volunteered to deliver meals on wheels. It was the kind of service that was satisfying and necessary. I visited convalescing hospital patients and patients who were dying. I looked around at Sunday services and saw dozens who were contributing many hours more, making genuine sacrifices. That broadened my respect for those often stoical folks, easily cartooned by cynics, who went to church every Sunday, sang the hymns, brought the food, and prayed for an ailing Emma of the congregation.

The Sunday services comforted me. It's true that the experience wasn't powerful enough to force me to look into the dark jaws of my alcoholism. And while they might have smoothed some of the hardest edges of my temperament, they produced no immediate miracles there. I could hardly blame a church service for that. And yet Sunday mornings became one of the most important hours. The week when I didn't hear Mark Hanson in the pulpit became a diminished week for me.

Some of the hymns captivated me. I remembered some of the old Western movies of my childhood, the black-and-white ones. It was obligatory for those movies to include a Sunday morning hymn-singing scene in the church on the hill. The choir included women, usually with long noses and plastered-down hairdos parted in the middle, and men with big shoulders about to split the seams of their Sunday coats. They would sing "Rock of Ages," and they nearly tore the roof off the fragile little chapel belting out the fervor of their frontier religion. So you had to be amused in the face of all that old-time religion if you were kid watching that movie. But years later in church, I came to love singing those old hymns in the green book. And on some mornings, the lyrics of one of them would cut through the walls of reserve and unspoken remorse I brought to church. They touched me with quiet forgiveness. Whatever the strifes in my mind about belief, I saw the words on the page, blurred by the dampness in my eyes, and heard in the voices around me the depth and simplicity of that forgiveness. They invoked the sacrifice of a man on the cross 2,000 years ago and what his agony had done for me. And I was unable to finish the hymn, "Just as I Am," because of my tears. The lyrics were saying I was accepted, just as I am. And then I would recall the words of another hymn, sung during the communion in another church when I was a boy: "O Lord, I Am Not Worthy."

But you are forgiven.

If you have sinned often and have felt the desolation of it, the thought of being forgiven through one man's sacrifice must leave you limp with thanksgiving. What act is there in our lives that is more beautiful than forgiveness? Human forgiveness or God's? Years before, in my newspapering, I'd met a woman at the request of one of her friends. The woman had lost her teenage daughter a few weeks before. Her daughter had been a passenger in the front seat of a car driven by one of her schoolmates. Her girlfriend had been drinking. She lost control of the car. There was a collision and a scream. And the innocent girl who rode with her, so lovely and vibrant moments before, was dead. Her mother, stricken in the days after the accident, still had the civility to take a telephone call from the girl who had driven the car. The girl spoke out of the depths of shame and helplessness. She did so again a few days later.

And then the woman who had lost her daughter to this girl's drunkenness and irresponsibility did an extraordinary thing. Knowing the family, she drove to the girl's home at night, learned that she was crying in bed, and walked into her room. She slipped into the girl's bed and hugged her. She said, "I forgive you."

When I sang the hymn in church, and choked on the words "just as I am," I recalled the woman, distraught from the death of the most precious person in her life, performing this ultimate act of humanity. She forgave—befriended—the girl whose recklessness had killed her child.

And on those days in and after church, days which seem so imbued with grace, I would have to ask myself a question: Why do you struggle so much and so hard?

Perhaps I can explain why.

My first exposures to serious churchgoing as an adult took place twenty years ago. My Sunday morning habits, as well as whatever small service chores I've been able to perform between Sundays, have not changed much since. Nor has the idea of private prayer.

That is part of the record. The other is that during this time I inflicted abuse on myself and emotional injury on others, the woman to whom I was married, my children and stepchildren, and others. When I drank, I lied, I neglected my children, and I kept running on an ever-accelerating treadmill of self-gratification.

It was a toll I refused to count for years. Two or three times I nearly died as a result of a headlong craving for excitement and goals that met my professional and personal ambitions. It was a craving that seems now to have mocked the other side of my person. That other side kept trying find some rhythm in life more durable than the thrills and pride that came from doing.

I wanted to say, "Hello, God, I believe. I love. I need to slow down."

Church and gospel and prayer would bring me closer, I said, make me understand more about the will of God, the entanglements of my own will, the uncluttered beauty of what Jesus Christ was teaching and demanding. That was what I hoped.

Did they?

It's been a siege. One recurring trap for me was the convenient disappearance of humility during large stages of those twenty years. Another was a habit of arguing with my will and not always being sure whether I ought to follow it or escape it. This internal struggle over will was complicated by my refusal to recognize God's. If I had to grade my maturing as a human being through the church experience, including what I think has been a genuine hunger to learn and to feel God's spirit and companionship, I'd have to call it this way: it's been rough and full of scars, but it's been better than it would be without the church.

For a lot of people, evidently, it isn't.

I am among the least qualified candidates on earth for the role of arbiter over which is the best road to personal peace. We live in a time when the information highway and the stresses of today's life have lifted the hunger for spirituality to the force of mania. It is, in fact, approaching a cascade in today's outpour of fixes for tense psyches and nerves.

Should we rejoice in this surge to discover the true key to spirituality?

Moderately might be a good way to rejoice.

Spirituality is a perfectly good word. It is a positive word.

It connotes depth of feeling that fosters serenity in us. It is a quality of being in contact with an ideal, with God, with a higher power or however the person who experiences spirituality chooses to define this force or spirit that puts one's life into a sphere of well-being. For some people it has nothing to do with God but seeks a harmony of being in this and only this world. Which means an atheist can rightly claim to have achieved spirituality. Most of us will see in it—or try to—something divine.

So let's say spirituality is peace. That is simple. It is recognizable. It is what I want and what took me an enormously long time and outlays of arrogance before I could honestly approach.

The problem overtaking spirituality today is that the idea is so good and attractive that it has been commandeered by the get-well-this-instant industry. As "The Answer" in our lives, it is being merchandised relentlessly. You can get spirituality in books, tapes, videos, and séances. This is good, old bottom-line capitalism. Identify a market. Serve it and hustle it. It's roughly the same treatment directed at other healthy concepts like "intimacy" and "openness," marketing that produced millions of dollars in profit by convincing hordes of people that their lives were barren unless they knew the secrets of intimacy and openness. We were invited to work them over in all of our idle moments the way we worked on Rubik's Cube. Intimacy was defined, redefined, dissected and enshrined. It achieved the highest threshold of the get-well vending by being packaged into working manuals.

Spirituality is too important to be accorded this fate.

A traveler on a tour with me a few years ago confided that he found his spirituality while staring at a flight of geese. I had no doubt of his sincerity. I did ask in what direction the geese were flying. I thought this could be a possible clue to a new direction in the search for inner calm. I want to thank God here and now that the guy had a sense of humor. The ensuing conversation might otherwise have been frosty. He laughed because, while he was yielding no ground in his enchantment with wild nature as the place where he drew his spirituality, he did recognize the oddity in deifying a gaggle of honkers.

My struggles to reverse my spiritual stumblings are blessed with no special wisdom, certainly no more than that of most people caught in the same fix. But I do try to avoid running from one "spiritual" antidote to another in dealing with my emptiness or misery. I'm convinced of this: Ultimately you're not likely to find the enduring peace—at least I'm not—unless it demands some form of sacrifice, some kind of surrender—surrender of ego, surrender of will, sometimes surrender of a lifestyle, of selfishness.

Smokers trying to give up the habit will probably concur in this. Notional cures, hypnosis and the rest, aren't likely to break the addiction. In the end, most of the people who have given up smoking have done it for two good reasons: the fear that cigarettes were going to kill them and the need to feel healthy again by not smoking. Both of those motivations demand facing the truth: Giving up tobacco isn't going to be easy. It requires sacrifice and a certain amount of psychological pain. But if you're going to stop, you simply have to stop, and you have to realize it is you who makes the sacrifice in creating this healthy new life of nonsmoking, actually saving your life. It wasn't a hypnotist or some peddler of painless cures. And that knowledge makes your resolve stronger. It makes your satisfaction greater and the release from cigarettes very likely permanent.

Which gets me back into the forest and the search for an honest faith. I thought I could connect with God by leaving the forest trail for a half hour and embracing the glory and silence of nature. Doing that, I found myself immersed in moments of contentment. But it was not enough to sustain the true union with God that I was looking for, the feeling of touching the goodness and love of God. It wasn't enough to green the spiritual desert I'd made for myself, the one in which I'd gotten lost.

There are no mind-stretching ways to do it. I once sat in California with a renowned spiritualist who years before sought to reunite the late Bishop Pike with his dead son. I did it as a professional assignment, but my personal fascination far outran the professional one. The appointment had been made by a friend in Minneapolis who told the spiritualist, George Daisley, nothing of my history. Mr. Daisley announced that I still revered my dead grandmother, which I did. He also advised me that my grandmother in spirit form was in the room that very moment; he could identify her and she extended her love. It seemed like the dutiful thing to return her greeting, which I did, concealing from Mr. Daisley both my growing fascination and my skepticism. But Mr. George Daisley then revealed the name of one of my mother's aunts. I did not know of my mother's aunt. I'd never heard my mother mention her. He said her name was Agnes. He could not have "read" my mind, because no Agnes was there. Later I called my mother and asked her if she could give me the names of her aunts.

One of them was Agnes.

That sent a chill whistling through me. My ignorance of the spirit world and the workings of extrasensory perception is monumental. I don't know what to make of the information George Daisley gave me, or whether the spirit of my grandmother was in that room that day.

None of it put me any closer to faith.

I then have to ask myself one more question: Where does this leave me?

It leaves me still drudging around in the narthex of the church on Sundays, admiring the grocery bags of pasta and cornflakes a couple of families just hauled in for somebody starving in Africa or hungry in West Virginia or northern Minnesota. It leaves me scanning all the sign-up sheets, the stubbornly upbeat quality of all the posters and announcements of youth sleigh rides, and wondering what blockbusters Isaiah has for us in the readings today.

Is this obsolete?

Remembering his friends' dismissal of church as a reasonable place to find their spirituality, the blundering churchgoer is left wondering whether his way of trying to fathom God still has value.

Well, I think it does.

I can only speak for one of the blunderers. Attending a communal service matters to me. Raising my voice in prayer and song in concert with hundreds of others (make that dozens of others on cold mornings in Minnesota) matters. We are together. We are different and some of us are aimless and some are mule-headed. Some are devout and some are automatons when they recite the Nicene Creed. And when the service dawdles and I scan the faces around me, I wonder how many of these people are as tormented as I am, how many are content with the level of their belief?

How many, if they'd lived in Nazi Germany and worshiped in comparable pews a half-century ago, would have met the commands of their conscience and lifted their voices about the bestiality they'd seen or heard whispered around them? How many would have been loyal enough to the creed of Christianity, and brave enough, to face reprisal?

Would you? Would I?

People in church. Human beings dealing with their fallibility. This is what defined those faces I scanned. But we were together. We were together as part of a history that, in the Christian church at least, began 2,000 years ago, and the songs we sing and the prayers we offer link us with those in the beginning.

I find that healing. The other comfort I find in communal worship, even deeper, is the Communion itself, the consecration of it, the receiving of it into my body.

I don't know of any moments in my life that are more solemn. If I knew nothing more about Christianity, if I had to spend the rest of my life agonizing over my belief or my lack of it, I could still cherish the moment of Communion as the transforming one for me. I cherish it that way not only because it removes a burden, if only briefly, or because it's a time when I feel true contrition and humility. But it is also the time when I am joined and whole. It is a moment when my brokenness is healed, the evil in me is forgiven, the ugliness wiped clean.

If that is not God's grace, what else is it? If I feel graced at this moment, why is it that I have spent most of my adult life vacillating between indifference and guilt and fantasy on the subject of God's existence? Those swings have been wildly erratic. They have moved from some private, melodramatic demand for actual evidence—as though this were a courtroom—to imagined encounters with God on a mountain ridge. Later, I put myself into private sessions of contemplation, trying to conjure God out of the air. Those exercises were my surrogates for faith. None of them got me much closer to it.

The reason is that I am a very human being with a mind that has a lot of holes in it as well as curiosity. It's a mind whose patron saint might have been Thomas. But about the profundity of receiving Communion I can't doubt my feelings. Something happens to me when I receive. I'm softened and cleansed. The world simplifies, and I give thanks.

But on some Sundays in those intervening years before the search ended I wanted to scream or cry because most of the others in those pews seemed content or reverential, and it wasn't coming to me.

And then I'd have to say: Are there others in this place who want to strong-arm their way into belief? And after I knock the gates down, peace will come gliding into my life in the quiet of night. Is that how it works?

No, it isn't. But I kept insisting that I will believe. I will have faith. I will walk with God because I want to.

The bulldozer at work, trying to power his way into humility.

Isn't that a sight? Recognizing it, I would feel like a mediocre stage actor, reciting lines without conviction, and I'd have to tell myself that I don't really believe. I was grasping for a relationship with God, but I hadn't found it in my brain, my heart, my will, or in my reveries.

And all this time I was rushing the clock in my other life,

working, running, organizing, writing, talking, and trying to find some flavor in that steaming stew of energy and self-expression. On Sundays I would slow down and try to reflect and find some calm. But some of that was a temporary exorcising of the ghost who kept rattling a chain in the back of my head, as though announcing, "Your need for excitement and to make something happen is bigger than your soul."

And once more I would ask, "Am I the only one flailing about this blindly?"

I wasn't. It only felt that way. So I decided to confront another sinner, a man who once preached and had made his peace with his unknowns and his past. I would ask him to show me the way.

6

Grace, Mozart, and the Man from Nazareth

The retired reverend lives in a tidy old gingerbread house in an eastern suburb of St. Paul on the fringe of the countryside, just off a neighborhood street named (what else would be right?) Little John. A small arbor of pines and maples in back of the house is available for contemplative moments. The house and the neighborhood present a mood of relaxed cordiality, which is what greeted me at the door when Bud Dixen answered the ring.

"I need to think straighter," I said.

The reverend said he was not overwhelmed with surprise.

His wife was off to her work in a care home. To be accurate about the Reverend Bud Dixen, he is semi-retired. On some Sunday mornings now, he serves as the designated shepherd for a group of friends who gather for a Bible study and service in their homes. He has been in my life for more than twenty years as friend, once as vulnerable and wayward as I have been, and now a kind of volunteer minister of reinforcement for me and for others adrift. He removed the ceremonial white collar years ago, which was good, because when he gets aroused talking about God or his social causes, or explaining some of his nonconformism, the swelling arteries in his neck threaten the collar's capacity. It was to his church that I went on that ugly morning when my drinking and promiscuity plunged me into the worst self-loathing of my life.

Bud Dixen is one of the more original thinkers I've met in my disjointed scrapes through the thickets of the spiritual life. I'd always found him droll but thoughtful. I respected his candor, his impulsive flights to explore the bafflements of life, and his lack of pretension. I'm not sure I had as much admiration for the buttoned-down black cap he wore in later life, giving him the look of an aging U-boat commander. But I did admire some small mementos on his study wall, remembering the days when he walked with Martin Luther King Jr. and his service in Korea. The reverend is one of those guys of serious calling who can't resist irony. This means he has to find room for some light comedy in any solemn talk of God-and-life. Sifting through my dilemmas, he rued some of his own. His life had survived almost as much personal turmoil as mine, and I liked his ability to examine it with the scopes of theology as well as his conscience. Which made his parlor a place to find some relief from all of those small implosions in my brain that passed for reflection about God-and-faith and why it had torn me up. This day was years after that winter morning of confession in his church. My pilgrimage had gained some ground in the intervening years. But it still left me a long way from milk and honey.

He listened to my recital of doubt, which by now had thinned out a little but had not dispersed. The sum of his response in the hour we talked gave me a lift. When I left it felt a little like Easter, the beginning again. Maybe it was because the guy was scarred himself and we had no secrets between us.

So he disposed of the appearances of tenderness. "Cool it," he said. "You may never get the answers you think you need. What makes you believe you're more bewildered than anybody else? What you may be is more hogheaded than most people in thinking there is one best way. Maybe you want the exact route with billboards fifteen feet high announcing that 'This is the way to peace.'"

It felt like Easter only temporarily. In addition to being candid, the reverend occasionally reveals unmistakable streaks of being a wise guy, enjoying a game of rhetorical fencing with his friends and guests. I bristled. Who said anything about billboards? Bewildered is not how I'd describe my state of mind on the subject of God. Fragile might be closer. The reverend put away his cutlery and put an arm around his guest. This was his house. The demands of courtesy put an end to the fencing. From his kitchen bakery bin he served an oatmeal cookie.

"Everybody is in doubt sooner or later," he said.

"Are you in doubt now?" I asked.

"About what?"

"About your faith and about God?"

"No. But there are lot of things that I don't know about it that others pretend to know. When I think about doubt, I go back to the scene on the cross. Here's Jesus Christ, nailed and hanging there and dying in terrific pain. In addition to whatever else he was and is, Christ was a human being. He's hanging there and he says, 'My God, my God, why have you forsaken me?'

"That was a cry of despair, from a human being. If the rest of us sometimes despair about being forgotten, feeling lost, you can't say we don't have the greatest role model."

The reverend said he thought that was instructive. He couldn't understand why more people in the throes of futility, doubting God, couldn't find it just as instructive. He said, "I've always been a little amused by the exuberance I've seen in the last fifteen or twenty years on the bumper stickers of people claiming 'I found God.' I have friends who are Jews who get the same kick out of it. One of them told me he was going to put a rebuttal sticker on his car that would set the record straight. It would say, 'We founded it.'"

So what's so amusing about claiming to find God?

"Well, I think it's usually the other way. God finds you. This is hardly an original thought, you know. It goes back a long way, and you can find a pretty convincing case for it not only in the scriptures but in watching human behavior and the mental acrobatics of people like you, sincere as they may be."

The reverend has one of those faces stitched with creases and lines, suggesting a certain amount of emotional battering in his own wanderings. It's the face of a duress from the past and a betrayal of personal trust not unlike mine. It was not the usual face of benign tutelage that you expected from stewardship in the pulpit and from pastoral work with two generations of sinners and sufferers. He was now happily married after a divorce of several years ago and torment for his family. When the reverend talked about pain and estrangement, from loved ones, from God, he was talking not only theology but from pain in his life, his own pain and that which he inflicted. From this minister you got no aloofness from the real world of human hypocrisy and atonement. And I don't know that he was all that impressed by my talk of puzzlement. I brought up Revelation, the last book in the New Testament. I said it sent me over the wall. I said it read like something Thomas De Quincy might have written in his first draft of the "Confessions of an English Opium Eater." My host shook his head brusquely. "Why?" he asked. "Why get yourself absorbed by your doubts? There is something of the agnostic in all of us, including me. Maybe a lot."

I was intrigued by the business of God doing the chasing.

"Well, think about it," he said. "Most people who want to experience that moment of revelation, or who just want to believe, have really been running away from God."

Why?

"Maybe because they're afraid to make a commitment to something beyond themselves, afraid of what they might have to surrender."

He dug out a copy of a poem written many years ago by Francis Thompson, called "The Hound of Heaven." He said almost everybody in the ministerial business eventually gets acquainted with it and is reinforced by it. It tells of the sinner on the run, exercising a frenzied range of strategies to evade a very energetic and, it turns out, very loving pursuer. The man on the run tells us:

I fled Him, down the nights and down the days;
I fled Him, down the arches of the years;
I fled Him, down the labyrinthine ways
Of my own mind; and in the mist of tears
I hid from Him, and under running laughter.
Up vistaed hopes I sped;
And shot, precipitated,
Adown Titanic glooms of chasmèd fears,
From those strong Feet that followed, Followed after.
But with unhurrying chase,
And unperturbed pace,
Deliberate speed, majestic instancy.
They beat—and a Voice beat
More instant than the feet—
"All things betray thee, who betrayest Me."

It was providential judgment, no doubt deserved, and it was some chase. The reasons the sinner fled were not hard to know. In his most intense longings he wanted to meet God, needed to and dreaded it. He wasn't sure about this God at all and didn't know how God's judgments would fall. He needed love, didn't deserve it, struggled with his unworthiness, but shrank from capitulation. The hunter was tireless. The pursuit carried across the borders of the earth, through the gold gateways of the stars and past the ports of the moon. The man on the run tried disguises and hiding places, tried to bluff his way past the sentinels and, in the end, exhausted, was overtaken and heard the voice of God saying:

Whom wilt thou find to love ignoble thee,
Save Me, save only me. . . .
Rise, clasp My hand, and come!

The poet's rhetoric was archaic but wise. It was both blunt and tender in sizing up human vulnerability facing the unknown of God. After I'd read the piece, my host asked if I recognized anybody in it.

I said I did. The reverend said he thought he recognized two people, himself and his guest, although he made the point that I was probably giving God a tougher race than he did and certainly making God breathe a lot harder.

I said I never saw it as a contest. I didn't have any intentions of getting into a long-distance race with God, and I wasn't going for any records. This admission earned me the last oatmeal cookie of the morning and changed the direction of our talk.

My own relationship with God, I said, whether real or imagined, was getting my lopsided attention. But it wasn't yielding any sunburst of clarity. I wanted to dig into the experience of others. The darkest sides of my personal experience couldn't have been the most hideous on earth. There had to be thousands like me. But there weren't thousands in the parlor with us. There were just two of us. In front of me was a man who'd fought in a war, walked the streets with civil rights leaders, made some horrendous mistakes in abusing his ministry, was an easily identifiable sinner but had made his acknowledgments and righted his life in his older years. In all that time he'd never abandoned belief.

I asked him what God meant in his life and when was he most aware of God.

"I'm most aware of God in a communal worship," he said. "People coming together to proclaim their love and belief is a big thing with me. A powerful sensation goes through me at times like that. I can almost literally feel the bond we share. It's the pilgrimage, but not only today's. We're people who are part of a historic, down-through-ages pilgrimage. At this moment of joined worship we're united with the millions who have gone before us and who will come after us. For me, that's a high and holy moment."

I told him that was an immensely appealing picture, being part of a great body bridging the ages, joined in common affirmation. I remembered the emotion I felt years before in the Roman catacomb. The difference between us was that the somewhat battered minister was a firmly enrolled, committed pilgrim. I was still looking down that track. He said it was wide enough for everybody and once again, as he had on that grungy winter day years ago when I sought the shelter of his church, he asked me to walk with him.

This was a lighter day. It was the kind of day when two people moving into their later years could banter about their inadequacies and their mixed views of immortality and remember the old wounds, now almost healed, wounds caused by their self-serving behavior of the past.

But the minister had healed better. And I was trying to find the way. I had to back up to his graphic picture of Jesus Christ hanging on a cross, atoning for our sins, my sins. Dying. This was the one single act that defines Christianity, its indivisible act. The Son of Man, the Son of God. Is that the one irreversible truth, I asked, Jesus Christ's deity, that you must accept to believe?

"Millions of people believe in God—Jews, Moslems, millions of others—without believing that Jesus was Messiah," he said. "You know that. Christians are followers of Christ, or try to be. They have to look at Christ's life differently than the others do. Why do you ask?"

I asked because my diggings in the deepest pits of my spiritual stress in later years somehow coincided with an outpouring of cover stories, essays, and harangues among popular periodicals and the Christian press challenging the bedrock Christian tenet, the divinity of Jesus Christ. Among the authors were Christian scholars, many of them caustically skeptical themselves. The ascension story, Jesus Christ physically soaring into heaven, looked fabricated, they said. The miracles were suspect and so were some of Gospel writers' mixed versions of episodes in Jesus' life. As a man trying hard to recapture faith, trying to nurture those childhood pictures of Jesus Christ the Redeemer in my efforts at worship, I found myself offended by the stridency of some of that skepticism.

The minister nodded.

As a journalist I understood the basis for it—the lack of evidence, the huge void in our knowledge of most of Jesus' life, the fairy-tale quality of some of those stories.

The minister nodded again, curious where this was going.

I said I banked all of this speculation and tried to sort it out. It went into a brain that already bulged with the testimony of others I'd talked to about their faith, how they achieved it, why and when it vanished, if it had, and how they look at Jesus Christ today. I said I wasn't sure at this distance whether all this interrogation was earnest probing to settle my own anxieties or an act of masochism. "Why put labels on it?" he said. "Go on." I recalled particularly a conversation with a woman I considered perceptive, one who attended church regularly. I asked her what she believes about Jesus Christ's divinity.

She said she doesn't discount it. But so much grew up around his life in its aftermath that she had trouble accepting all of it. The trinity of God is simply hard to grasp, she said. So is the literal picture of Christ's ascension. I asked if the idea of God is just as hard to conceive. "No," she said. "I believe in a loving, mysterious God. I believe that the word of God and the inspiration of God came to the peoples of the world not only through the grace of God but through prophets and holy men who spread the values of good life here on earth."

Prophets like Mohammed, Buddha, and Jesus Christ?

"Yes."

Are we then to call Jesus Christ one of the prophets or the Son of God?

She said she didn't get all snarled up in her life trying to make the distinction. The greatness of Jesus Christ, she said, his immortality and the movement he founded with his preachings, the way he lived and died, altered the course of civilization. It changed forever how people live. In the time in which he lived, people slaughtered each other routinely. Human value didn't amount to much. Here came this man in simple garments offering a code of living that must have seemed alien to his times. He said love and care for one another. We are together. If somebody or if life gives you a blow, you don't have to retaliate. Love not only the ones you're supposed to love but your enemies as well. All of them are loved by God. Knowing that we can be weak makes us stronger. Get rid of your material riches. Share them with the poor. Walk with the poor. Eat with the poor. Eat with sinners. There's sin in all of us. Be kind in how you act and think, and you will find peace in your heart.

That was her summation of Christ's message. I asked the minister if it was his.

"Sure it is. The new hysteria among the scholars about whether Christ was divine or simply a man for all ages is fascinating to me, but it doesn't change my life or my faith. I think a Christian should probe and question and search the boundaries of his or her behavior to find out how they accord with the codes of Christianity. But I believe in God. Jesus Christ is part of that belief as the revealer, as conscience, as the one who redeemed us. That's my faith. Let the scholars haggle over the rest."

I said I would try. His words created a broad umbrella: It gives you freedom to think and inquire, which I was doing. But the umbrella can't stretch beyond limit. Eventually the logic of your inquiry may just force you to step out into the rain and to look for a new spiritual identity. The woman I talked to said the umbrella stretches far enough. "I believe there's a God, that God is everywhere in my life and on earth. Some people might say my belief might be a form of humanism. I don't care what they call it. I'm comfortable worshiping in the Christian church, and comfortable calling myself Christian."

How many, I asked Bud Dixen, occupy common ground with this woman, and do it sensibly? And why wasn't I doing the same?

He didn't have to answer. I wasn't doing it as easily because my obsession with doubt was sand in my eyes. It was irritating and worrisome. I'd now moved past my middle years, and I was either going to need a bigger umbrella or walk out into that cold rain.

Dixen was through with umbrellas. "You asked about awareness of God," he said. "I think I'm more aware than ever now when I hear beautiful music or walk through a gallery and find one of those British landscape scenes done by a gifted artist. You've seen them. There's countryside that seems untroubled. It's soft and introspective, so inviting that you're instantly drawn into it. The gift to produce truly beautiful and lasting art, or to write or play great jazz, is the gift of God, I'm convinced. Not all art is going to hit you that way. And you don't have to be an art critic to recognize it. But there are simply times when I see something divine in a painting, and I tell myself, 'That is the touch of God.' I don't say that glibly. I really feel it and I really believe it. Consider how much time we spend bitching about the world we live in and about our lives, being offended by what the politicians say or how much money the jocks make. We're ticked off by injustice. That includes the big injustice that condemns so many people to being shut out of the comforts the rest of us enjoy routinely, or the small injustice of the snubs we get in the marketplace or from knuckleheads who just don't appreciate us. We probably don't blame God for that, although we're doing a pretty good job of it when misery piles up for us and we wail, 'God, why me? Why me?'"

"Reverend . . ." I started to interrupt. This sounded like a prologue to one of his more protracted sermons.

"I'm making a point about recognizing God in our lives," he said. "We look at beauty, created by the hand of man or woman, or the beauty that a lovely spring day can put into our lives. That beauty makes us better, for ourselves and for those around us. We don't often think that here is a pure gift to us, that it is God's grace enriching the day for us."

Only a clod is going to offer a serious rebuttal to that idea, clods and maybe a few hundred million nonbelievers and pantheists and related thinkers who do not necessarily attribute a lovely spring day to the hand of God. To many who see God and nature as identical, a lovely spring day is God and, having said that, they can dismiss all the theological wrangling.

The conversation with the reverend was too fruitful and amiable to allow any serious degeneration into wrangling. I decided to walk the road with him for the few minutes remaining to us.

And where does it end?

"What?"

The road. What comes after we leave it?

"You mean life after death?"

The same.

And so the talk got to what comes after the grave, after the boilerplate eulogy and the inheritance tax assessors. Heaven is often a tough nut for the seeker-in-doubt to swallow. Hell is even harder. The reverend said he couldn't care less about how we define them.

"If you're talking about whatever version we have of heaven or hell today, I don't know if the places we've created in our minds exist. I try not to get bogged down in that quagmire. I think it's irrelevant to having faith in God and loving God, and being loved by God. In deciding how I live my life here on earth, trying to understand my relationship to God, what happens after I die doesn't cause me any sleepless nights."

He offered this view affably, as though the wisdom of his thesis was so self-evident that it yielded no serious dissent. Nobody knows about heaven and hell one way or another, he was saying, so why sweat it? Since I'd come to his door in the garments of a theologically ignorant truth-seeker, I let it ride. But I must have looked quizzical. He explained.

"Look. One of the great gifts we get from God is the right and power to exercise a free will. Within limits, we can choose to be good or bad, educated or dumb, generous or greedy. We can accept or reject ideas, and we can look at Christian teaching with an open mind. So when the argument gets to the hereafter, I pretty much bail out. I don't know what if anything God intends for us after we've put in our time here. Most of us grew up with a picture of hell as some kind of eternal bonfire, Dante's *Inferno*. I don't buy into that. I don't see checking in with Saint Peter at the golden gates, either, and going over my sin book with him. You'd think heaven would be something different. But if there's nothing after we die, it wouldn't alter my faith. And my faith tells me that if we're supposed to be provided for after this life, God will provide. I just don't think about it or worry about it, and I know for a mortal certainty that how we act here on earth, whether we act like bastards or saints, isn't going to make any difference about where we go after we die."

I gave this free-wheeling monologue the thoughtful silence it seemed to deserve. Here was a man who dished out Christianity to praying sinners on Sunday morning, most of it safe and by-the-book yet also practical here-and-now Christianity. But here he was declaring ignorance about a place so fixed in the tradition of worship that it's usually our introduction to God as children and the last word in our requiem when we die.

"I'm not saying I don't believe in a heaven," he said. "I just don't know what it is or if it is."

"Is a belief in heaven, the hereafter, pretty core stuff in Christian teaching?" I asked.

He said it probably is. He preferred his own word.

Which is?

"Call it a mystery."

The theology class in the parlor, the word according to the reverend, was drawing to a close. His final ideas were these: "A lot of people who are Christians still are stuck on the idea that if they perform good works here on earth, feed the poor, shelter the homeless, all that, they are following some blueprint on how to get to heaven. They may be good folks, and that may actually be motivating them, but if it is, it's the wrong reason. When we're performing a service to the needy, acting out of our purest and most generous impulses, what we're really doing is acting out of thanksgiving to God and out of love for God. It shouldn't be because we expect some kind of reward."

So the maverick preacher was safely back in the stable. What he had spoken at the finish was good, hard-rock Lutheran theology, and I congratulated him on finding his way back. The workings of the trained and pragmatic Lutheran mind in the pulpit have fascinated me—as a transferring Catholic—from the time I became one of the churchgoing regulars. The Reformation freed these folks to inquire, to democratize worship, to debate theology *ad nauseam*, and to recycle an endless carousel of synods. Yet one of the more benevolent parts of the ecumenical movement, it seems to me, this closer cooperation among the dozens of separate houses of Christianity, is that it gives Protestant ministers a chance to get a little more comfortable with the more appealing parts of the early church without surrendering any of the ground won so resoundingly by Martin Luther. The historic linkages of the Roman Catholic Church are part of that appeal: some of its mystique, some of its language, a little of its pageantry. That is the Church of Peter, in other words, in all of its historic might and romance.

And yet nobody who speaks from the Lutheran pulpit is going to mess too creatively with what Martin Luther was all about. Lutheran preachers bear down on the principle of unconditional grace and reconciliation by faith tirelessly. They do it gently or stoically; they do it with scholarship or with humor; but they do it. Some of them are chagrined when they see evidence that good and sturdy Lutherans in the flock still look on the doing of good (hauling those grocery bags into the narthex) as a measurement of their Christianity and therefore the salvageability of their souls.

No, no, comes the admonition from the collars. It's great to do good. The world needs it. The church needs it. But God's forgiveness and blessing aren't connected with it. Please know the difference.

Well, I think the collars are right. But what do we make of all this?

Probably that the old-time religion dies hard and it sometimes can't let go of the old formula, that our behavior decides who gets rewarded and who gets punished. The instinct to think that way collides with the theologians, who know better. Sympathize with the theologians. It's a hard world for prophets and wise men.

The minister and I parted. He'd given me a new attitude if not a new direction. You can conduct the struggle for God, try to find some sensible tenor of life that makes God a vital part of it, without bleeding or ripping yourself apart with all the dangling pieces that don't seem to fit. An occasional laugh at your own intensities wouldn't hurt. He gave me that. He gave me something more.

He didn't say the existence of great art was proof of God's grace moving in our lives, enriching them. He simply said there is great and enduring art, and it is a gift in the hands and mind of the artist, and who else but from God?

Driving down the freeway on my way home, I keyed in the car's CD tray and listened to Beethoven's Violin Concerto. So here was beauty in my life, great music. As much as it has meant to me, I'd rarely been moved to thank God for blessing my life in this way. My friend with the oatmeal cookies had implicitly posed a question: Why wouldn't you?

If God created earth, whether by loosing a big bang or by moving an impressive amount of dirt and stardust in six days, it means he gave to the human senses a receptivity to beauty with which he would endow the earth. To my friend, that was self-evident. Less devout critics would argue that the Beethoven violin concerto now filling my automobile flowed from the composer's genius and sweat more than from heavenly grace. Isaac Stern's violin in the CD player was too elegant for me to get involved in that particular brawl. Nobody has to convince me of Beethoven's genius. But take that further. The word genius itself defines as gift. From where and whom?

The highway traffic was light. I drove and listened and nodded. I remembered all of the times in my life when music touched me so powerfully that I found myself as close to a transcendent calm, or an ecstasy, or contrition as I would ever be.

What was there in the music? Whose presence was in it?

The most moving music I know is the "Kyrie," the first passage, of Mozart's *C Minor Mass*. I can't listen to this music, or see it performed, without weeping. Music affects me this way. It affects me especially when it summons an image of the purest unselfish love, or of sacrifice, or when it makes a plea for forgiveness; or when it reminds of a loss. When the hymn "Spirit of God," is sung in our church, it is hard for me to get through the words, "Stoop to my weakness, strength to me impart." It is a hymn of tenderness and commitment, and it was sung as part of my wedding service in 1980. When it's sung today, I remember that hour, the loveliness of it and the commitment of it, and then my folly in destroying the promise of it, and I have to close the book because I can't go on singing. Still, I love the hymn and its consolation. Great music can give sound to all of those feelings and qualities. And yet even when this sound is expressed in what we call sacred music, I don't think I had ever consciously thought of it as a gift or benediction.

The reflections of my friend the minister moved me to think of it now. Why did I react to Mozart's "Kyrie" as I did? Well, here was an invitation to dig into my psyche and those elusive tappings of my emotions and conscience. There had to be more in this music than Mozart's mastery of musical language. In my video collection is a performance of the *C Minor Mass* given in the Abbey Church of Waldsassen in Bavaria in 1990. The orchestra is the Bavarian Symphony. The massed voices are those of the Bavarian Radio Chorus. The soloists are among the finest of the European and international concert stage—Frederica von Stade, Arleen Auger, Frank Lopardo, and Cornelius Hauptmann, conducted by Leonard Bernstein.

Kyrie means Lord. The "Kyrie" of the service is a plea for forgiveness. In Greek, "*Kyrie eleison.* Lord, have mercy. *Christe eleison.* Christ, have mercy." In the performance in Bavaria, the soprano, Arleen Auger, stands before the audience-congregation, the surrogate for all who seek absolution, speaking their contrition. As she begins, the basses of the orchestra tread slowly and solemnly in affirmation, and then the massed voices join the soprano's voice, and the church is filled with the cry of humanity itself: *Kyrie eleison.* Lord, have mercy. Have mercy on us.

Arleen Auger's voice descends with great tenderness. She is the pilgrim in need, expressing humanity's need: *Christe.* There is a pause. The chorus and orchestra are silent. The voice then lifts and soars into a cry of supplication and calls once more, "Christe!"

Jesus Christ.

Help us.

Each time I experience that moment, I find my shoulders pitching involuntarily, and even in privacy I'm somehow embarrassed by the intensity of the emotion, although I don't know why I should be. A picture works itself into my brain. A man is hanging on a cross, losing consciousness. Christianity says this is true man but also true God, and he lived among us to redeem the sins of humanity, and he is so human that his last words are "My God, why have you forsaken me?" But he is dying. And as he is, here, in the voice of the great chorus, is humanity calling his name. It peals across the gulfs of time, pasts the tempests of hatred and strife, and embraces his message of peace and forgiveness. It is a voice united in trust and hope and need.

The scene of Golgotha in my imagination merges with the music on my television screen. Leonard Bernstein closes his eyes, overwhelmed. The music recedes, and the "Kyrie" is over.

What was real? What happened?

What was real was the transforming power of the music, giving voice to humanity's pilgrimage and its vulnerability.

What was real was the passion the music created. What was real was the sorrow and the thanksgiving I felt.

What also was real was one small voice, mine, making an admission. There was so much about this that eluded me, and so much with which I'd struggled. But at that moment of wonder, I felt the embrace of something beyond me.

The reverend calls that grace.

I don't know a better word.

7

Waves of Crisis

The idea of death did not substantially horn in on my thoughts through the first sixty years of my life. What was the rush? Death was something unlovely that hung around with the insurance man's actuarial tables. It could wait until the next millennium. When I was ready to start reading the scare stories about Social Security drying up, I could start thinking about death.

My timetable for taking death seriously suddenly moved up in December of 1992 at about the time I was slipping into oblivion from the anesthetic on my way to a quadruple bypass surgery. And although I could not be aware of it, what lay ahead in the next six months approaching my sixty-third year was a chain of medical and personal traumas that would put me on the edge of destruction, change my life, and eventually open the door to God.

Until then, dying was not an option that merited my close attentions. There were times when it had been near, in the mountains where the possibility of death should always be part of the climber's psychological preparation but rarely is. More than fifteen years before, a climbing partner and I lost the route on a relatively easy climb in the Grand Tetons and found ourselves on a perpendicular rock pitch with meager holds and a 2,000-foot exposure. My partner reached for a rock knob, and he came off. He slid down the rock face, gaining speed, and yelled, "Falling!" Where I stood I had only a half-inch ridge in the rock for a finger hold and only enough rock underfoot to stand on my toes. It couldn't have been enough to withstand the shock of a falling body on the rope joining us. More as a fatalistic gesture than a serious attempt to save us, I looped the rope around my arm inside my elbow. I had two or three seconds to do my farewells. I didn't pray. I didn't think about God. It was happening so swiftly I didn't feel fear. What I felt was sadness. It was too soon to go, and it was such a futile way to do it. I braced for the end, which didn't come. The rope around my arm, amazingly, held my partner. It burned into my skin and took some blood, and the rope marks are still there, but the rope held the two of us on the mountain face. I don't remember thanking God when it was over. I was that obtuse about life and death, and so estranged from spiritual feelings at the time.

I'd been less estranged a few years before in another mountain accident, on a snow mountain called Huascarán in the Andes. My partner, Rod Wilson, was suffering from what turned out to be pulmonary edema, a high altitude sickness in which the lungs fill with blood. In his weakened state his crampons lost their grip on the ice and sent him hurtling down the mountain. I jammed my ice ax in the snow, wound the belay rope around it, and leaned into the ax. The rope came taut and stopped Rod after he'd shot out over a crevasse. The guide-porter and I led Rod down to our camp at 19,000 feet and tried to make him comfortable. The gurgling in his lungs was an announcement of imminent death unless we either got him to lower altitude or produced some oxygen.

He was in no condition to descend through the ice field. Fausto, the guide, set out in the dead of night for an oxygen cylinder we'd stashed below the crevasses at 14,000 feet. I tried to keep Rod awake in his sleeping bag with talk and hope. He was remarkably calm and courteous, but not over-whelmed by the conversation. After an hour or so he said he had a pocket Bible in his down jacket, lying near his sleeping bag. I dug it out and asked what he would like to hear. Rod was a man of faith. He told me to use my own judgment. For two hours I skipped through the New Testament, reading the stories of Christ and the admonishments and wisdom of Paul. I thought it prudent to ignore the book of Revelation. From time to time we'd talk about the passages. It became a Bible study in the Andean night wind at 19,000 feet. He stayed awake, sounding thoughtful and comforted. At daybreak Fausto's brown face thrust itself through the tent flap, followed by the green oxygen bottle, which saved Rod's life.

Or did it?

What saved him? Was it the green oxygen bottle or the consolation and strength he received from the words he heard in the night wind? Was it a combination of those, or was it, after all, God's will? And how do we identify God's will? Months later, I asked Rod about it. He said there are things we don't have to know, but for which we should offer a prayer of thanksgiving. It was an answer that might explain his calm in the face of threatened death on the mountain, and might also explain his survival.

Until my sixty-fourth year, those were the moments of my exposure to death. Neither shook me into a conscious examination of my mortality or made the approaching footsteps of God any more audible. My heart surgery was the start. My notions of invincibility may have begun to vanish with the appearance of the hospital chaplain in my room a few hours before the bypass surgery. He asked if I cared to pray. Well, yes. Prayer seemed a reasonable act under the conditions. The day before, the heart surgeon had walked briskly into the patients' lounge at Abbott Northwestern Medical Center in Minneapolis and had given me a briefing of the next day's operating agenda. The surgeon was small and athletic. His neat little mustache gave him the appearance of some surgical Alan Ladd. He also happened to be one of the best heart surgeons in America, Bob Emery. His speech was frugal. "Aside from the lousy heart arteries," he said, "you look in pretty good shape. Your chances are excellent. We'll be operating for several hours. Good luck."

"Tell me," I said, "more."

He said the four big arteries of the heart were clogged from 85 to 100 percent, which made me a walking death notice unless they were cleared up. The blockage resulted primarily from age, from the cholesterol buildup from what I ate, and from stress. He didn't inquire about the source of the stress. He was wise enough not to ask. Listening to the reply might have kept him in the patients' lounge for a week. During the operation, he said, the arteries would be cleaned out or replaced. My heart would be stopped, its functions performed by a machine. The heart itself would be encased in slushy ice.

"It will have the appearance of a large frozen daiquiri," said the surgeon.

If the surgeon is as nimble with the blades as he is with metaphors, I thought, I ought to be the picture of health in two days.

A day before the bypass, the cardiologist had produced a chart identifying the blockages. He followed with a short monologue required by the hospital attorneys. While there was every likelihood of a successful operation, he said, there was a remote possibility that I would die on the operating table. The possibility of heart muscle damage was 15 percent and the chance of a stroke 1 to 2 percent. My body's generally good condition outside of the blocked arteries, reduced those odds, he said. This was helpful. I asked what were the odds of loss of toenails. He said the mortuarial charts were silent on that.

I don't mean to be frivolous about the heart surgery or the complacency with my health that led up to it. But you can bury yourself in grimness if you look too hard at your probabilities on the brink of a big heart operation in your sixties in the face of a life of alcoholism and self-imposed tension. There was one other thing. I was confident. I was confident in the surgery, in the quality of Minnesota's medicine, in the hospital and its staff, and in the high possibility of success.

So when my daughter Amy held my hand as I rolled toward the surgical room, and Mark Hanson prayed quietly with me, I expected to emerge healed in five or six hours. And it happened that way. The surgeon cut open the breastplate, retooled me with a new arterial system, transferred one of my leg veins to the heart as part of the bypass, and reassembled the split sternum with metal stitchwork. My heart, spared by the wonder of today's surgery, resumed work and, in three weeks, so did I.

As a price of the pace I'd lived in the past twenty years and some of the recklessness of it, I'd have settled for the bypass surgery. But events at the time were beginning to crowd my life with grief and alienation. A few months before the surgery, my second wife, Lois, filed for divorce. She said she did it with regret, and I'm sure she was truthful. Our marriage of twelve years was both tempestuous and fruitful, although we were separated as much as we were together. We mattered to each other and had shared some marvelous times on the trail and in the hours when our clashing temperaments didn't derail our mutual fondness. Her complaints centered on my periodic drinking and what she said was my chronic refusal to speak candidly with her about problems of our relationship. Some of our most fulfilling interludes, as I remember it now, where the times when we attended church together. She visited the hospital during my post-surgery convalescence and, as a trained nurse as well as estranged wife, insisted on reporting to one of the examining doctors that it might be a good idea to check my PSA reading, which is a marker for the potential existence of prostate cancer.

He did. The reading was high enough to warrant a biopsy. The findings were negative. I relaxed and made a trip to New Zealand. They took a second biopsy when I returned, three or four months after the heart surgery. Half of the sixty-six cells they examined were malignant.

When I was a child in the mining town, a diagnosis of cancer was a sentence of death. It was so much a diagnosis to dread that nobody talked about cancer or identified it that way. Instead, it bore the whispered short hand of "the Big C." It wasn't much different elsewhere in the country. Families refused to identify cancer as the cause of death of their loved ones, as though having it and dying of it were too devastating to share with the public. Medical advances twenty and twenty-five years ago began to change that. Cancer could be detected early. Certain kinds of cancer could be slowed, then stopped. Eventually, almost all forms of cancer—if they had not advanced to the terminal stage—could be treated in some measure to give the patient prospects for a lengthy or normal life.

The doctors said, "Yours ought to be removed."

What ought to be removed?

"The cancer, along with the prostate gland."

What does removal of the prostate gland mean?

"Probably continued life. Do you find any serious alternatives to that?"

We got into the standardized macho anxieties about restricted sex life, but the conversation was more or less overwhelmed by the absurdity of it. Men can have their prostate glands removed and still have a sex life in one of several forms, most of them perfectly satisfying. And even if they don't, do you seriously want to wager against the best medical advice?

The operation was performed successfully. Four days before it was, the trauma deepened.

Seven months after the divorce papers were filed, five months after the heart surgery, and less than a week before the cancer operation, I was arrested for drunken driving.

It happened in a little town west of Minneapolis while I was driving home after reconnoitering the route of the annual bike ride I organize for members of my adventure travel club. I'd like to plead stress over the impending cancer operation. I can't. I sometimes drank when I was on the road. It shortened the miles, I decided.

The real reason was that it gave me a high, a lift. Did it matter that this was criminal conduct when the drinking got past two or three, endangering innocent people on the road?

I could manage that. I could control the car. When I got into speed zones, instinctive wariness would take over. I'd slow down.

The local police officer saw that. He also saw the erratic movement of the car as it wove over and around the yellow lines in the street. His rotating lights appeared in my rearview mirror and I drew up to a curb.

He was polite. "I think you've been drinking," he said.

I nodded. He gave me some coordination tests. I flunked. He then drove me to the police station and administered a test for blood alcohol content.

I was over the limit. He wrote a citation charging me with driving under the influence of alcohol and asked what I wanted to do. I was legally drunk but close enough to sensibility to feel the shock of what was happening.

I'd created this scene: father of two grown women, age sixty-three, prominent local journalist, fitness enthusiast, and self-designated conscience of the community, is sitting in a small-town police station, revealed to be drunk, a highway menace to defenseless people.

I called my first wife, Rose, who drove from her home in the middle of night to deliver me to my house. She didn't lecture. She didn't judge. She came as a friend and because I was the father of her children, and she cried. By then my head had cleared to the point where I could feel the oppressive shame for my reckless act, for putting this good woman through her own grief in the face of mine. I was clear enough to consider the extraordinary generosity of her act. We'd been divorced for nearly twenty years, and she was weeping to see me in pain and to foresee the humiliation that would follow.

There was nothing trifling about the humiliation. Because nothing was more important to me that day, and because I owed an accounting to the readers of the newspaper, I wrote my column about my drunken driving arrest. I said I was doing this not because it was a self-serving attempt at therapy but because it was a devastating experience for me that justified the shame I felt and because it laid bare what I'd refused to accept—that I was an alcoholic. It had nothing to do with my impending cancer operation, I said. But because of the drunken-driving episode and because of the uncertainty tied in with the operation, this might be my last opportunity to write. I apologized and asked for the readers' forgiveness.

The newspaper placed the column on the front page. The gist of it: well-known journalist, adventurer and conscience of the community, is a drunk by his own admission and by the evidence of more than twenty years.

The cancer operation followed a few days later. During my four days of convalescence, mail began arriving by postal sack. In the end, there must have been 7,000 to 8,000 letters. Almost all of them voiced some form of support. Many of them were uncompromising in damning my act. It was, they said, foolish, inexcusable, and criminal.

They did not say it was unforgivable. At the time, I'd written my newspaper column for nearly thirty years. A trust had grown up, I think, between writer and readers. Most of them thought they understood my personality, its quirks and attitudes, and whatever generosity of spirit they saw in it. They'd read my stories from political convention halls and athletic arenas and the hospital room of a dying old war hero. Some days they laughed with me, and other days they snarled at me, and some days, I suppose, they ignored me. But for the most part they'd welcomed me onto the doorstep of their homes each day, and now and then they might put me on their refrigerator door. However they reacted to my political twists or my tastes in cliff hanging, they got accustomed to having me around the house. And I think they realized—whether or not I'd written it publicly—that the energy for my column came from the most important relationship I had in my work, the one with the newspaper's readers. Their letters in the aftermath of my arrest and my admission of alcoholism reflected their willingness to continue that relationship. I felt their kindness and loyalty. God, they were needed. They gave me warmth, made me feel privileged to have earned the friendship of those who'd written them. They were offering me their shelter. Some of them were also offering their acidic wisdom, which might have been worth as much as the friendship. "Just because you pontificate about politics and take us to wild parts of the world," one of them wrote, "doesn't mean that you can't be as dumb as anybody else."

My daughter Amy might have given me more love but somewhat less charity. I tell you about it because to be fruitful and truly worthwhile, our lives must center on the most important relationships we have, on those we love, and I'd squandered or neglected some of those relationships. But the one I had with my older daughter had been strong and constant. It was bonded by the interests we shared in social justice and politics and spiced by our difference in temperament. She had a gift for making friends and keeping them, and an easy, social gracefulness that tended to cushion a flinty mind not afraid to make hard decisions. She was three years older than her sister, which brought her into the adult world sooner. That meant that she was strong enough to undertake long-distance bike rides with her father, events that seemed to stretch the growing distance between her younger sister and me. I could have avoided that. I didn't work hard enough or creatively enough to do it.

Thoughtlessness is another word that comes into my mind now, but might not have then. Whatever the reasons, the life of my younger daughter, Meagan, moved down a much harder road. It led her to drop out of high school despite an IQ at least equal to that of her sister, who became a lawyer. It led her to years of personal heartbreak and dead-end jobs that demanded nothing from her untapped mind. And then, after more than ten largely aimless years and at the age of thirty-four, she entered college—and filled her report sheets with 4.0 averages. We began to have long and searching talks about what had gone wrong between us, how our nearly identical personalities practically decreed that things would go wrong between us, and how much space there was in our two lives for reconciliation.

We didn't talk about God's grace bringing us closer to common ground. I didn't bring it up because the two of us together were still so fragile that in some ungainly way I wanted to credit her with making it happen. Obviously her decision to change her life and to pour her energy into that change was at the center of her transformation. But I also know there was another, unseen, presence in that particular miracle, and I don't forget it now when the day is done and there is time to consider the bounty in our lives.

But Meagan was hundreds of miles away at the time of my drunken driving and the operations, and Amy was close at hand. After she'd walked at my side to the operating room for the cancer operation, she was waiting in the reception room of an evaluation center where the counselors would determine if my drinking history warranted treatment for alcoholism. She was there as a daughter who loved her father and had shared thousands of miles with him on the open road, giggled and wept and dodged tornadoes with him. She was also there as a witness for the victims of my drinking, herself included. But she was fundamentally there as a prosecutor.

And she came with indictments.

I listened to the proceedings lying on my back. The spinal I took for my operation produced an aftermath of pain when I stood or sat. The body hadn't sealed itself where the anesthesiologist had penetrated with his syringe, causing some form of drainage that produced severe pain when I took any position other than supine. If you'll excuse a pretty wild digression: The anesthesiologist, a highly respected one, happened to be from my home town on the Iron Range. His father and I had worked together as young men before leaving for college. When I reported the pain, the anesthesiologist was embarrassed. "In 95 percent of those spinals," he said, "there's no trouble afterward. A few patients get what you have. I might have made a mistake in where I entered the anesthetic. I apologize, and let's fix it." I said it was perfectly understandable, and I bore no grievance whatever. The first fix, meaning an attempt to seal the opening, didn't work. Neither did the second. I telephoned from my home again a few days later with the unhappy news. He sounded exasperated. "You may or may not appreciate this," he said, "but let me ask if you drink coffee?" I said I do. "Make up a pot of extra strong coffee and drink it the rest of the day," he said. "You might even consider two pots. The reason I'm suggesting this is that caffeine sometimes works in these cases where the finest remedies known to modern, miraculous medicine can't seem to do it. Try it." I drank two pots of coffee the rest of the day and the next morning. That afternoon I sat up for three hours reading. Not one twitch of pain invaded my body. I've never understood why I haven't read about this amazing medical breakthrough in the *New England Journal of Medicine*.

But the caffeine came after the hearing in the evaluation office, which was part of the court proceedings. Was I sick enough, in my drinking, to need strong and disciplined inpatient treatment? The clinical psychologist in charge of the office would decide after examining the record and hearing testimony, mine and that of my daughter Amy. Neil Riley, a retired judge I'd known for thirty years, drove me to the suburban counseling and evaluation center a few miles from my home. Riley was the kind of friend who, although a judge, made no judgments of his friends. "What they're going to tell you," he said, "is probably going to be the best thing you could hear." There were four of us in the office, whose furniture and lighting reflected a sensible compromise between warmth and business, suggesting to the examinee: This is not a lounge. That's not why you're here. This was an examination that would give the judge information he needed to decide on things like the penalty for DWI and treatment for it. I lay on a recliner. The counselor sat at her desk. Mark Hanson sat next to Amy. He must have known how hungrily I welcomed him. This was going to be an ocean-going keelhauling, and it was good to see at least one life raft on the premises.

I don't know that I'd ever told this man what he'd meant in my life, that no one apart from my family had influenced me and moved me spiritually as he had. At every crisis in my later life he was somewhere in the scene with his prayer and what I had to call his Christian demeanor of constructive gravity. It was written all over his long Norwegian face when the doctors or the judge approached. Or he was there in my face, this time gently, with his nurture and his friendship. Mark Hanson knew about Christ, and I didn't. Mark brought into my life as no one else has the message of the Christian ethic, with all of its hope and all of its down-and-dirty demands on social conscience and personal honesty. He preached a Christianity of pain as well as promise. If you really believed what Christ was saying, he said, you could still play golf at the country club and party with the neighbors and diddle with the stock market. But there had to be a part of your mind and soul that prodded you to stretch your community into the streets and the prisons and the kitchens for the homeless, into the loneliness of the misfits of society, into the angers and the yearnings of people who are different sexually. If you could not reach into their communities or offer yours to them, he was saying, you were not hearing Jesus Christ. At first glimpse, here was a formidable guy, Mark Hanson. He was tall and bearded and had that seminary-sculpted, ministerial look of chronic burden. But most of that rubbed away at some stage of his sermons, into which he usually threaded some self-squelching episode from the supermarket or the family living room. If the Gospel for the day was hard and unpalatable, he didn't come with sugar and cranberries. Trying to live the creeds of Christianity some days meant tough decisions, walking on sharp rocks, trying to understand and forgive a thief or a cheat. If the Gospel was befuddling, he shared his befuddlement. But he usually found his way through the scriptural mists in time to make the listener feel relieved to find glimmers of light at the finish and for being able to breathe a little easier, thank God.

I don't mean to be nominating this guy for the Mighty

Fortress in the Sky. When he was younger, he riled the college and seminary authorities with his street radicalism (not necessarily bad, either the street radicalism or riling the ecclesiastical crocks). Screaming matches with the kids in his house were probably not unknown. But he brought the search for God alive for me in the sixteen years in which he was my pastor in two churches. Nobody I've met so personified and expressed the Christian ideal in his uncompromising witness in his daily life. He became a bishop in spite of those unblinking commitments to social and human justice that disturbed the frostier members of his several congregations. He became a bishop not only because he preached powerfully but because he had a corporate savvy for problem solving, for church management, and for building bridges among urban communities where historic suspicions and outright hostility had existed.

I doubt that he got most of that directly from God. He got his evangelism, shaped for the mentality and chaotic pace of the twentieth century, from his evangelist father. But he got his realistic feel for the human condition in equal dosages from the street, from Scripture, and from the tumult of raising a multiracial family of six kids, four of them adopted.

But I'd confided to him once that what wise ministers needed most was an unerring judgment in knowing when not to sound wise. The reverend clearly had acquired that judgment. In the evaluation center that day, he sat silently and glanced at me before the testimony began, looking sympathetic, as though we were members of a secret society that wasn't going to enjoy hearing what was coming next.

It was a gut cruncher, what came next. Amy was going to be satisfied with nothing short of an in-patient treatment center for her father. She was a lawyer, and she came to prosecute, but her goals weren't the conventional ones of the prosecutor. Her objective was not to force a confinement on her father, but to free him from a tyranny—alcoholism—to which he'd willingly submitted. Her objective was not punishment but healing.

She wasted no energy either on an opening argument or on being kind. She recreated a scene out of the living room of her childhood.

"I don't know if you remember the night of my birthday when I was a little girl," she said.

I asked her to help me remember which night.

"You walked into the house two hours after mother and Beth (which is what we called her younger sister then before she changed her name to Meagan) had eaten dinner. We had my birthday without you. The candles were still stuck in what was left of the cake when you came home drunk."

She didn't say those blown candles were witnesses to the embarrassment of the evening. But they were.

I said I remembered the night.

"I don't think you remember all of it," she said. "You came home without a present. You also came home looking and smelling awful."

I asked her to tell how the evening ended.

She didn't sound vengeful. She wasn't. She was a composed young lawyer, in her early thirties, remembering an awful scene from her childhood, speaking quietly. But her calm couldn't conceal her disgust recalling that scene.

"You tried to apologize," she said. "You tried to hug me. You had too much to drink. You lost your balance and we both fell into the couch."

I did remember the rest of the episode. The child had more class than her father. Instead of running off in tears, she laughed and threatened to ground me for forgetting her birthday. She said it would be OK if I took them to a Vikings game. And what was she doing? She'd been hurt by my grotesque behavior. She'd seen my ignominy. But with her laughter she was offering to forgive in the ways kids will when they are trying to salvage the worth of a derelict parent who has lost some of their respect but not their love.

Lying on the office recliner, I flinched listening to Amy's recital. She said nothing of her compassion that concluded that living room scene. But she began to stoke up her anger over the repetitions of it in later years. At one stage I shook my head as though making a private rebuttal: But those were episodes out of my worst years of drinking. I didn't drink for four or five years after that. Isn't that right?

She might have read my mind.

"What were the worst years of your drinking?" she seemed to be asking.

I came half-fried to her graduation party, too, at Rose's home, two years after our divorce after twenty-two years of marriage.

She spoke of the neglect in their formative years, hers and Meagan's, a neglect whose damage I was either too busy or heedless to recognize.

"It wasn't what you did when you were drinking that hurt the most but what you didn't do," she said. "There was almost never a family night at the movies."

Yes, we had vacations in the mountains. Fun. They were so much fun, I heard Amy saying, that they magnified the huge vacuums of time that I could have devoted to their mother's interests, their progress in school, and the routine trials of growing up. And for those, there was almost never an affectionate arm from their father or some sensible advice. I just wasn't there enough.

She got up from her chair in the counselor's office and walked toward my couch.

"I think you loved us," she said. "You didn't act that way because you were callous. I don't think you were. It was the alcohol."

Booze. Booze for a lift, booze for a tonic, for escape. Escape from what? Escape from being a father?

She moved up the time frame. After all of that, she said, I hadn't learned.

"Do you remember the drive you and I took to your mother's in Ely?"

I did. She was a lawyer by then, an adult, a friend of the court. My daughter. Twice on that day she'd cautioned me about my loose driving conduct. The third time, she yelled.

"I don't want to ride in this car if you're going to drive." I offered the usual arguments. They rolled off her building furies. "If we're going to get there," she said, "I'm going to drive."

I yielded the wheel. No conversation ensued for the next 150 miles. When we got to my mother's place, she spared me the expected homily. Her manner and voice were free of judgment. "We both know you need some help to get you out of this," she said. "You're better than this. Please do it."

I said she was probably right. I said nothing further except to apologize and ask her not to worry.

Then she was a fretful daughter. Now she was in the evaluator's office, bringing a case. She recounted the evasions I had worked on the same trip to northern Minnesota. The morning after we got there I went out to the car trunk to get what I described as spare clothing. The young lawyer watched the performance from my mother's living room window. I returned without the spare clothing. "I saw you duck your head into the trunk and sip something," she said.

Alcoholics are notorious for their alleged cunning when trapped.

"Mouthwash," I said, "I forgot to bring it into the house."

"It smells like whiskey," she said.

I said this was probably the power of suggestion and that she was just plain wrong.

In the evaluation office she told this story with a notable absence of compassion. She did it with painstaking detail and in a tone that expressed both her rage and her terrible dismay in the face of her father's refusal to accept the truth and to accept his obligations as a father and as a man whose public visibility made him a figure of trust to many who read and heard his words.

She finished her witness. "People still believe in you, and so do I," she said. "But you could have killed somebody driving drunk. You could have killed yourself. You're an alcoholic. Why do other people have to tell you that? Why does the law have to tell you that? What does it take to make you see what you're doing to yourself?"

She walked to my couch. Here eyes were clouded, and she looked distraught. When she got there she leaned down to me, gave me an embrace, and kissed me on the cheek. "I love you," she said. "I hope I didn't hurt you. I had to speak."

Her words left me lying mute and shredded but oddly thankful. Amy's testimony had filled the circle for her and for the rest of the family. Words that could have been spoken years before, protesting words, words of injury, were now on the record and had pierced my past delusions about meeting my family responsibilities. I actually had talked myself into believing I had met those responsibilities. A forgotten anniversary here and there and coming home in time for the evening news now and then, grabbing a sandwich and flopping into bed. That was my night with the family.

The evaluator wasn't strapped by indecision in making her recommendation to the court. If anybody in town needed treatment to change the course of his life and to head off predictable disasters down the road, this one did.

Why am I dragging you through this melodrama of roadside arrest, shame, and confrontation?

I'm doing it because many of us may have a mutual interest in that bizarre flight from God, the actual fear of discovering God, that I've been trying to document here. We may have a mutual interest because others have launched themselves into the same kind of flight. Perhaps you have, or someone close to you. It's a familiar spectacle, but the soul who's running almost never defines himself or herself as a fugitive from God. The scene in the evaluation office, my daughter delivering a chronology that laid bare my failures as a father and my slippery behavior as a user, forced me into my first serious decision in ending the flight.

I slowed the pace of it. I must have asked, "Why am I running, from what, and where am I going?"

I didn't know enough at the time to tell myself I was running from God. What I was running from, I said, was truth.

Either way, the answer would have been right.

8

Man on the Run, Meet God

The celebrated English author Oscar Wilde wrote a book in the late 1800s entitled *The Picture of Dorian Gray*. It is a story of personal corruption, the dehumanizing toll and deepening ugliness of it reflected in the changing face of a portrait of a wealthy young man who devoted his life to pursuing pleasure and perversion at their most grotesque. As it was originally painted, the portrait depicted a young man of remarkable good looks and delicate features. The subject of it, Dorian Gray, soon plunged into a life of depravity, prowling the London sinkholes and netherworld. From time to time on his return to his manor from his nocturnal roamings, sated and bemused, he would glance at his portrait. To his amazement, he began noticing changes in the face—a curling lip, hardened eyes. An illusion, he thought. But as his conduct worsened, the face began to alter itself radically, turning itself into a mask that appeared vile and fierce and finally monstrous. He was forced to hide the painting in an upstairs room behind a curtain and locked door. Finally he brought the painter to examine it, satisfied now that some unknown force of judgment had twisted the face in the portrait to mirror the evil of his life.

Seeing it, the painter was stricken and disbelieving. Yet he was able to recognize his original brush strokes. He recalled the original elegance in the painting. "There was nothing evil in it, nothing shameful," he mourned to Dorian Gray. "This is the face of a satyr."

Dorian Gray corrected him. "It is," he said, "the face of my soul."

Dorian Gray was observant but notably without remorse. He eventually killed the painter and, crazed by the mocking bestiality in the picture, drove a knife into it. They found him a few hours later, a knife in his heart, the face in the portrait filled with its original beauty.

This is an artful piece of writing, Wilde's only novel, revealing an imaginatively acidic mind at work. But what's it doing here?

The Picture of Dorian Gray, the movie I'd seen as a youngster and the book I later read, came edging back to me one afternoon in a small treatment center for chemical dependency in a rural town north of the Twin Cities in the spring of 1993.

Please accept that I was no Corn Belt version of Dorian Gray. Dorian Gray was a fictional demon, without conscience, invented for the purposes of telling a horror story. I was one of millions, an ordinary, run-of-the-road sinner trying to bumble his way toward betterment in the face of the familiar impediments of character stains. These included, but were not confined to, selfishness spliced with regret, plus most of the usual suspects of the alcoholic mentality—evasiveness, grandiosity, random belligerence, and defensiveness. To these could be added a mucked-up spiritual side.

God, wasn't there anything in that benighted litany of fault to yield some light of decency?

To be even-handed about it, there was. I had virtues of loyalty and compassion and outcroppings of tenderness. I could extend care to the forgotten and a voice to the powerless. I could love, although I didn't do it well. I delivered on promises, returned my calls, worked an honest day, and kept my obligations—none of which erased the darker side of my own portrait, or explained what I was doing at the age of sixty-five on a spring day in 1993 in a treatment center amid cornfields, trying to absorb the chalked writing I was staring at.

A dim image of the Dorian Gray story slipped through my troubled head, not because the message on the blackboard in front of me revealed the disfigurement of a soul, mine, but because it revealed the disfigurement of what could have been a better life. On the blackboard in front of me were notes and descriptions covering five columns. They had been written in white chalk by the counselor conducting the session. The words were mine, drawn by the counselor during his interrogation. They represented a dossier of my drinking history and its results, showing the cycles of drinking and sobriety, random drinking, accelerated drinking, and the assessed damage of it. The columns were headed: Age. Drugs Used. How Often. Amount Used. Consequences.

I was seated in front of the blackboard in a semicircle with six other members of the group, all of them forced into treatment by court order, as I was. Two of the others were young men in their twenties, their drugs of choice marijuana, hash, and cocaine. Another was a woman making her ninth attempt at recovery. The others were adult men, trying to extricate themselves from the alcohol traps. One was the middle-aged son of wealthy parents, a knockabout on the beaches and in the casinos of America, alternating between booze and cocaine to keep himself hyped up. All of them were serious about recovery. The beach dweller was thoughtful and remorseful. I gave him a strong eight to stay sober when he left. He did. He's a counselor today. And what were the chances of the aging newspaper columnist fresh from the cancer ward?

My chances depended entirely on how I read what I saw in white chalk, whether I was serious or unconvinced about my alcoholism. If convinced, I had to decide whether I had a will tough enough to stop drinking, or needed other arms and other voices to do it. All of my history of drinking told me there aren't many wills that tough. Mine wasn't the exception. Cigarettes I could stop and did. Booze no. But right now the best candidate to provide the rescuing arms was the unseen one I'd been eagerly trying to escape for most of my life.

"We came to believe," recovering alcoholics tell themselves, "that a power greater than ourselves could restore us to sanity."

I'd read it a hundred times, and recited it once in a speech to a group of recovering alcoholics, fifteen minutes after drinking a double bourbon at the hotel bar. That's how deep I'd buried personal honesty. I'd read it a hundred times, but I doubt that I ever believed it. Alcoholism bends your brain that way. It dupes and ambushes. Using alcohol had loused up large chunks of my life. I knew that. I also knew that some day I was going to have to walk away from it or be torn away from it, or die from it. But there were years when I did no drinking, or seven- or eight-month stretches when I did no drinking. It's over, I'd said then. I don't need it.

I didn't really mean that. In the midst of my self-congratulations for staying sober, I managed to keep the door cracked open to make alcohol handy in a crunch or when a good time seemed to demand it.

But on this afternoon, the white chalk on the blackboard had put me at a junction in my life where I probably would not stand again. My instincts were prodding me with that warning, practically shouting it. Look hard and deep at what you see today, man, at this moment. Do you recognize yourself? Do you understand now the destruction you have caused?

The bookkeeping was on the board, stark and inescapable, written in the counselor's hand but drawn from my own deposition. It was the first time I'd been exposed to a full accounting of thirty years of drinking, the intermissions of sobriety and contrition, denial of drinking, rumpus-with-the-football-players-and-politicians drinking. Drinking in the morning. Drinking alone.

The last column was the one I dreaded. It told of the damage, first to personal honesty, because drinking led to infidelity and deceit. The damage expanded. My daughters' lives were damaged because of my thoughtlessness and by the days and nights when I was simply invisible, nowhere to be seen. My marriages were damaged and the second one destroyed by my neglect and by the lies and distrust. My stepchildren, Lois's daughter and two sons, one dealing with diabetes, were damaged by my aloofness. How? I didn't get involved in their schooling. I went to some of their games and plays, but it was a loose pretense at commitment. They saw that. I told them how much I admired them, because they all revealed high character, and I meant it. I didn't say "I love you." Withholding. Being distant. God, why?

The losses mounted. Three times before I'd been stopped for suspected driving under the influence, but each time the lawyer managed a reduced charge because the reading was marginal. But the insurance companies hardly ignore the court reports. Drinking began costing thousands. My first divorce, from Rose, cost both parties additional thousands. My second divorce cost more. The bookkeeping ran into the hundreds of thousands spread over twenty years. An accident in the 1980s piled on more thousands. Slowing down to observe the scene of an arrest at midnight on a suburban highway on my way home, I piled into the rear of another car. A second arrest followed. Mine. I'd been playing poker with a Las Vegas character named Amarillo Slim for a newspaper column the next day and had a few drinks. They weren't enough to sustain a DWI charge. They were enough to inflict injury, thankfully minor, on the driver of the car in front of me. They were enough to produce a civil suit that cost the insurance company $20,000.

They weren't enough to end my drinking.

At the finish, the counselor was about to run out of board space. The final damage in the 1990s, at least as registered on the blackboard, was the second divorce, tens of thousands of dollars lost in the settlement and attorneys fees, a $700 fine on the DWI charge, two days in the workhouse, and thousands of dollars in added insurance premiums.

The cost didn't include the public embarrassment my acts had inflicted on those who loved me or the menace to the lives of drivers on the road. Finally, the counselor said, "There's no category for the damage that you have done to yourself. Would you agree with that?"

It was the only judgment, or implied judgment, he made. The rest was etched in chalk.

I stared at it, overwhelmed. The room was silent. There was a muffled shifting in seats. Nobody could have been shocked. All of them had been through their own versions of this self-convicting horror. They wanted to be sympathetic. I could feel the unspoken, awkward solidarity in the room. If they weren't in shock, I was. The counselor stood at the blackboard, looking into my eyes, trying to be generous. Finally, in a voice as soft as he could make it without sounding sympathetic, he said. "What do you think?"

I couldn't answer. I didn't want to be discourteous, but I couldn't release my mind or my eyes from the scene of destruction written on the board. When the recital was over, I closed my eyes and the small voice of the sympathetic advocate spoke to me from my reeling brain. "That's not all of your life. There's some worth." But it wasn't on the blackboard. What was there was a hideous indictment of the worst parts of my life. I searched it for some summation of this thirty-year-chronicle of recklessness and for the spiritual poverty it revealed. I found it in the last entries in the column of consequences:

Age 50-56. Disruption of second marriage and inability to have close relations with stepchildren. Alienation of some friends. Lying to protect addiction. Occasional blackouts. Mostly drinking alone.

Age 60-65. Wife filed for divorce. Drinking occasionally, almost always alone. Drinking while traveling. Arrest for DWI May 1.

The counselor was waiting. He did not seem impatient.

I lowered my head and closed my eyes hard, twisting my face behind my cupped hands, creating some kind of futile contortion to express my revulsion. Trying to obliterate something. The room. The lingering gaze of the counselor. The pitiless verdict of the blackboard. Or my own verdict. I'd lived with communication all my life, but now I wanted to shut myself away from the inquiring counselor, but not run. I wanted to face myself alone, to be alone, to cry alone. I had never felt such terrible devastation.

I was alone. For a moment. I remembered part of the language in "Amazing Grace," the passage about "the hour I first believed."

This was the hour for me.

It wasn't opening a door and saying, "God, I'm helpless, against the wall. Now I believe. Come on in."

A deal.

No, not that. I don't think God is into conversion by negotiation.

What I believed first, at that moment, were the truths of the silent judgment on the blackboard.

The first truth was that I was alcoholic.

The second truth was that today, at this hour, I accepted the fact of my alcoholism.

The third truth was my helplessness to recover from it without the embrace of a strength greater than mine. That meant submitting. Tough, worldly guys aren't supposed to submit. They do it their way.

I submitted.

This was the hour to surrender the arrogance that convinced me I could control an evil and drain the alcohol from my life with my will, logic, and chutzpah. I would say, "Time to stop. It's getting embarrassing," but it didn't stop because all my defenses were bluster and facade, a con game with myself as the perpetrator and victim.

I'd gone down that road before. I could control. Events. People. Booze. But my will was the will of convenience. It walked out when the thirst for booze got in the way.

But the message on the board in those slanting white letters of the counselor's hand was not only about alcoholism. It was about a man trying to power his way through life, gratifying himself, burning his energies, going to the ends of the earth, trampling his own peace and that of those close to him.

It was about a man traveling alone in the middle of the crowds that were part of his life. He was alone because he lacked the humility, couldn't finally bring himself to believe—without smothering in doubt—in something, someone, beyond him, someone in charge of the mysteries that confounded him, someone who could bring the peace and beauty to whoever was ready to accept it.

The counselor cleared his throat.

I looked up and apologized for my silence. I said I had just looked into a mirror and it left me numb. It exposed the seamiest side of my life in a way that tolerated no denial. It had shown me the truth as I had never pictured it and as I had refused to picture it.

It wiped me out. I didn't want to talk any more. I didn't want to reach for the alternative, either, by declaring my remorse in the ways you do—shaking the head and breathing deep to acknowledge wrongdoing. Whatever I could say or do seemed empty and theatric. I just wanted to leave there, not to escape the blackboard but to wring out my mind. I asked if we could look deeper into my history tomorrow, because I needed some time alone. The counselor nodded, and I walked to my room. The casino dweller who later became a counselor and my friend clamped his hand on my shoulder and squeezed it.

I closed the door to my room and knelt by my bed.

I didn't pray. I knelt motionless, trying to gather myself, too stricken to whisper or speak. I didn't pray because after all those years of pretending, I didn't really know how. I didn't know whether to confess, to bawl, or to ask for mercy. I was choking with disgust. I knelt by the bed, craving some kind of relief.

All that was there was the late sun in the window, settling slowly through trees.

The sun in the country, normal and comforting, as familiar in the landscape as a barking dog and leaves twitching in the breeze. In a few minutes sunlight brushed my face. It was my first sensation of warmth in two hours.

It was the beginning of relief. I opened my eyes and squinted into the orange and genial blob, slipping through the young maples, free of the intervening branches and now glorious and innocent and full of nurture. Effortlessly, the blossoming countryside had turned itself into a painting: the world slowing down to enjoy a spring evening in rural Minnesota. I was surrounded by it and gaping, but something about this picture of the universe seemed changed.

A man kneeling by his bed is not the likeliest nominee to be the center of this universe. I'd not always been bashful about running for that particular office or about feeding on the illusion. Me, at the center. Godzilla and his agendas for today. Nobody could entertain an ego that breathtaking, but I don't know that I ever ran away from it, either. After the beating down of the last two hours, with reality boring into me all that time and dissolving my alibis and rationalizations, the notion of me at the center of my universe seemed so amusing it was worth a smile. So I smiled at the comedy of it.

I stood and walked to the window. Maybe it was the smile that eased the choking in my throat and slowed the pounding of guilt. The afternoon had dumped a thousand anvils on my head. Each one of those statements of charges was a sledgehammer ringing on the anvils. But in the waning sunlight, in my solitude, I felt some of the pain and loathing spilling away. I was breathing normally again, released from my emotional gagging. The disgust had lifted so that I was able to speak to myself for the first time.

"I won't go down that road again," I said.

I would never pervert my life again as I had allowed a drinking addiction to do it. That was the vow. It's what I thought I was telling myself. But I can honestly tell you now, in the hindsight of five years, that those words of commitment—minus the macho defiance and rumblings of willpower I would have used in the years before—were spoken as a plea. I didn't recognize it at the time. They were meant to break down a wall of isolation. I'd built it myself, the wall isolating me from God. I'd fortified myself from God because I'd never had the modesty to submit to the will of God or to the love of God. God was a wonderful idea, but there was too much mythology about God and too much in unsolvable riddle. God could be embarrassing. How many times had I listened to a jock reciting his good fortune for his fifty-yard touchdown run by giving thanks to God, when it was his speedy legs and the fullback's block that looked more instrumental to me than God?

I wouldn't accept that this guy might be utterly sincere in his belief. I didn't accept it because post-game avowals like that sometimes get to be show biz. So I wouldn't or couldn't understand what this one was saying as joyously as he could: his speedy legs were a gift. They were a gift from God, and he wanted to give thanks.

Belief—the relationship with God—had to be more complicated than that. I'd built a fortress and locked myself inside to protect me from simple acceptance. I did it with the images. God was icon and stained glass. How could God be reality?

The fortress became a dungeon. How could God be reality when my one reality on that day was my degradation in a treatment center in the country? I'd just seen the evidence of my duplicities and my limitless skills and urges in the field of self-destruction; that and my capacity for abusing those who loved and needed me or trusted me. The evidence was irreversible. It covered a whole blackboard and half of my life.

God came back into my life on that day.

For several years afterward, in the times I would offer thanks for the reunion, I assumed that God had obliged a man suffering in his helplessness and walked back into his life when he whispered: "God help me. I can't do this alone. I want to believe. I want to get back to the truth."

But I know today that what brought God into that room in the treatment center was not only a cry of despair but my exhaustion from running. Here was a place where I could no longer hide. My flight ended with a simple admission. I was powerless alone.

Francis Thompson called God the Hound of Heaven, the stubbornly pursuing God. It took him a while to break down the walls. But finally, they gave way, and the Hound of Heaven might have said to me in that room in rural Minnesota what he told another fleeing soul:

> How little worthy of any love thou art!
> Whom wilt thou find to love ignoble thee,
> Save Me, save only Me?
> All which I took from thee I did but take,
> Not for thy harms,
> But just that thou might'st seek it in My arms.
> All which thy child's mistake
> Fancies as lost, I have stored for thee at home:
> Rise, clasp My hand, and come!

I felt cleansed. My alcoholism had been a sickbed where I'd been trussed for years without realizing it. I refused to recognize it until I was too weak to leave on my own. When I admitted the truth to myself, and to those who were my witness, the healing began.

It began that day. In the twelfth step of the code of Alcoholics Anonymous, a program filled with the recovering alcoholic's connection with God or what's called a Higher Power, there is a reference to "spiritual awakening." It is left to the recoverer to define this spiritual awakening and the time when it comes.

And now who and what do we have? Here is a man who underwent an experience so powerful in its effect on one critical part of his behavior that it led him to reexamine the entire fabric of his life, to see clearly what he could never bring himself to see before.

What was different about the view now?

The clouds of self-deception pretty much had to collapse and dissolve. When they did, new definitions of old attitudes and behavior had to emerge. What I once confidently called "energy" to explain my furious schedules and pursuit of goals now looked and sounded very much like "ego." Not bad, perhaps, but more accurate. What I once called "pride" now surfaced under the more revealing label of "grandiosity." But if I could now see how self-deception had fed some of the colossal mistakes of my life, I could also look at the worth in my life less defensively. When I drank and found myself arguing with my wife about my failures in all those impressive categories of the domestic scene—intimacy, openness, attentiveness, and the rest of the familiar cast—I would counterattack by parading my virtues. I turned into a scorekeeper. I might have a tendency to withdraw and stonewall, I said, but I wasn't abusive. I might not be the toast of the reunion of in-laws, but I always arrived on time and I met my promises. When the dialogue took this turn, it was usually demeaning. It almost never ended the argument.

But in the room in the country in the descending sun, the argument seemed about to end.

My other voice did not abdicate when I began recover. It prodded me into another interrogation.

Did the watershed day in the treatment center suddenly transform your personality and, with this new vision, put you on the road to tranquility?

No, it was a beginning.

Of what?

Of a rediscovery of honesty.

Honesty in what?

In my relationships. In defining my attitudes and behavior. In trying to change the ruder and self-serving parts of it.

Are you running for sainthood?

I would have lost on the first ballot. I'm running for a more faithful way to conduct my life and to understand my place in what I can now call God's world.

So you actually believe that experience in the treatment center was an encounter with God?

I do.

There I dialed out the other voice temporarily but probed that question. Yes, God was in the room, but that is hardly a revelation, is it? Most who believe today accept that God is everywhere. Granted that most of our images of God and His whereabouts are still largely the residuals of our childhood, reinforced by the language of the Bible, reinforced by a hundred billion sermons for 2,000 years, reinforced by the movies. God is in His heaven. What could be more normal? What could be handier for a millennium's worth of poets and painters than a picture of God delivering judgments from the clouds. Where would Michelangelo be without God in His heaven?

God may be in His heaven, but if He is, God also has to be a roamer. When you accept God, you have to accept that proposition, don't you? You have to accept and believe that God is not only in heaven, whatever its geography, not only in the sanctum behind the glowing red lamp in church, and not only hovering over the casket at funerals. If you accept God, you have to believe that God is on that quiet trail in the forest but also in the honking congestion of the street. In other words, this is the world of His creation, and God is here.

Is God perched on our shoulder, kibitzing or warning us?

Well, I doubt it. What I think about God in the world, in our lives, is that God is available. "They say that God is everywhere," Emily Dickinson said, "and yet we always think of God as a recluse."

Yes, but not always, Emily. When we are desperate enough, isolated and lost, we don't think of God sitting solemnly on this throne, making judgments. We don't ask for a judgment then, or at least I didn't. I asked for mercy. I didn't see myself standing in some celestial queue waiting for a verdict. I saw myself as afraid and helpless. And that is the time when we pray to a God who is in this room, "Please, God, come into my life."

Whatever images we carry of God don't much matter alongside our needs and the intimacy with the spirit of God that most of us crave: The feeling of walking beside God or Jesus Christ, confiding and sharing, drawing strength, is an irresistible one to people wrestling with confusion and grief in their lives.

A few days after the day of the blackboard, I went for a walk in the spring sun along the lawn at the treatment center, and I segued back into my conscience one final time before being discharged into the real and suspenseful world. One more interrogation, I said, and then maybe you will be closer to whole. What I really wanted to know was: Am I ready?

Is that idea of walking with God a poetic daydream, piling your load on him, confiding your fears? Or is that kind of relationship possible?

Five years ago, I would have said it's pretty much a fantasy, trying to romanticize a relationship with God. I don't say it now. It goes back to the blackboard and what entered my life in the hours after.

One of the things that entered my life was a truth voiced by an old man speaking at one of the A.A. meetings at the treatment center. "We're only as sick," he said, "as the secrets we keep."

I'd been keeping secrets from everybody in my life, from those I loved, from myself, from the priest in the confessional, trying to keep secrets from God.

And what have you learned about God?

About God, what do we—what do I—really know except the need to trust? We can accept what we read in the scriptures or not be convinced. We can embrace this gospel or reject it as fiction. What we really know about spiritual experience, about our relationship with God, is what is happening in our lives.

Did you need some kind of revelation for that, an event?

I might have. There are millions of decent people who are guided by a lifelong belief that keeps them open to the joy of knowing God is near. All of their lives they've been comforted by this nearness in the face of pain. But an event did occur to me. A discovery I made, a truth to which I submitted. It rescued me from a swamp that seemed bottomless.

How did you feel then and how do you feel now?

I felt a liberation, an unburdening. It set my life in a direction that has brought me closer to personal peace. It didn't instantly transform ugly into beautiful, murk to sudden clarity. It moved me toward a place others wiser or luckier than I am had found long before.

And that is?

To a feeling of ease knowing that there is in your life a spirit that is generous, close, and companionable.

And you call that spirit what? A Higher Power?

I call it the grace of God. It didn't come in dazzling light. There was a quality in it that caused me to stir. Something about me that moment was different, and I think is different now. I felt something benign, something I would never want to lose. I didn't feel anointed. What I felt was acceptance. What I felt was a baptism, this time as an adult. There were no murmurings by the minister. What I heard was internal: "It's time to get back to the truth."

The examination was over. I walked back into the treatment

center, sorting out some thoughts about faith and grace. The theology of today is that we are forgiven or justified by this grace of God, through faith, or simply through grace. No strings about it, no deals. We don't have to tithe or run through walls to get to church on time. We receive because we are human and we need. But to open this great reservoir of grace to us, Jesus Christ had to die on the cross to give us atonement and reconcile us with God. We respond with faith and the love of God because we are grateful.

Does one necessarily follow the other, grace followed by faith? "Luther used this comparison," one of my ministerial friends said. "A man in his wedding-night bedroom, naked with his naked wife, doesn't have to make love to her. But why wouldn't he?"

I like that story. It offers me as much light in connecting grace and faith as it does in discovering the origins of the Lutherans' reputation for having practical minds.

My personal reconciliation happened to be connected to my overdue admissions of alcoholism. You can call it disease, addiction, weakness. Choose the word. It brought me to the edge of catastrophe before I confessed my helplessness to control it. That confession, the acknowledgment, brought God back into my life because it forced me to see the wisdom of the Twelve Step creed of Alcoholics Anonymous, which is meaningless unless the recovering alcoholic recognizes a being greater than self, a being who will direct life when it becomes unmanageable to the one trying to stay sane.

The conversions to faith are hardly confined to people who can't handle the booze or drug habit. They spread across the whole prism of humanity in need or adrift. Others can experience that moment in the quiet of their living room or on a walk to the grocery store. Others may not experience it at all. They may simply have been receptive to a quiet change in their lives, and offered a door that said, "Welcome." The gift they received is the same.

The rediscovery that deepened my life most was the simple beauty and power of prayer. I prayed robotically for years, like a kid giving his wish list to Santa Claus. After a while the words didn't matter. If God was that compassionate, he was going to cut through the raw insincerity.

But now I began to actually lay myself open, to talk to God through prayer, a small greeting in the morning, thanks for the safe night, for one more day of sobriety, for what's better in my life, for listening when I ask for help or guidance for myself or for others.

The calm in my life came slowly. Honesty came imperfectly. Faith came after years of floundering.

But they came.

9

How Do You Love an Unseen God?

The changes in my life didn't lift me abruptly into the enchanted forest. Sainthood was even further out. There's something about the routine roadblocks and muddling of daily life that is at odds with uninterrupted bliss. Those sputtering fuses in my personality that gave me a push toward alcoholism and the spiritual drift that went with it weren't extinguished in one spring day in the country, momentous as it was for me.

But I don't want to minimize the changes.

I gained a willingness to face the truth. It meant the rediscovery of the integrity I'd lost.

I gained sobriety. It meant being able to deal with my world and my realities with a clear brain. It meant being able to shed the alibis and evasions that hobbled my personal relationships. It meant bringing the zany round-the-clock action of my life down to manageable speed.

I gained reconciliation with God. It meant putting the core of identity back into my life. It simplified life's purpose but expanded its possibilities. It restored a trust in what lies ahead, replacing a frenzy to comprehend it.

What I feel most strongly in prayer today is gratitude for where I am and who I now am. I translate gratitude into being able to receive God's love and to return it. I don't do it perfectly. I sometimes ask myself, "How do you love someone, something, you can't see and can't feel?" And it is then that love and thanksgiving become interchangeable for me, and the question is answered.

Prayer, yes. But, if you don't mind another question, to what kind of God do we pray?

The question is serious but maybe it ought to be recast. When I say, "we," I may be rash. Whose God? Yours or mine? We may not visualize the same God. In a simpler time of worship, if you believed in God, you formulated an idea of God. You may even have decided on God's disposition. You almost certainly decided on God's location. All of that tended to make a straight line of the connection with God, the relationship. Today, we learn, that might be naive. Today, squadrons of colliding theologians battle constantly over the identity of God, the form of God, and the power and validity of prayer to God.

In the cerebral style of today, many of these people, attempting to be both reverent and relevant, are trying to adapt theology to science—the changing dynamics of new science, the dynamics of man's relationship to the universe. So we live and pray today in a spreading tanglewood of new conceptions of God, wrapping themselves into the more traditional attitudes of what God is all about. It used to be paradise and Judgment Day and all of that. Today's proposition—a faceless God, without vocal chords, a God without physical dimension but a God who is simply there and everywhere—unhinges some of the traditionalists but gives others an energizing second wind. I may be one of them. This is God as spirit; God as grace. That may be closer.

There's an irony in the widening debate over the nature of God and of heaven and about the existence of God. The squabbling is wasted on most people, at least in my experience. Basically, people adhere to tradition. This means personalizing God, making God a benevolent monarch, imagining heaven as a reconstituted Garden of Eden beyond the sun. Those ideas are implanted in the big majority of believers, and they stick. For most people who are satisfied with them, belief becomes the lifeblood of hope. It grants trust and humility and inspires thanksgiving.

Is something wrong with that?

Nothing. Without these, life isn't worth much. It wasn't for me. For all those years, I'd lurked and fumbled on the edges of faith. A different life, with faith at its center, began when I had enough sense and enough desperation to accept grace into my life and to identify the wellspring of it.

And yet it wasn't until very recently, when I sat with my ninety-year-old mother in her room in a care home in Minneapolis, that I fully understood the transforming power of simple prayer for one who has given a lifelong trust to it.

My mother had lived alone for nearly twenty years in the small home in which my younger brother and I grew up on the Iron Range. My father died of leukemia when he was seventy-four. He was the provider and patriarch. Mother was the nurturer and healer. She was a tiny woman of energy and managerial skills in the house. But under the rules and manners of the times, she was dependent on her husband, followed his lead. When he died, she mourned for months, visited his grave constantly. Relatives were convinced that with her husband dead and her children gone, my mother was going to shrivel into helplessness.

She didn't. Nor did she abandon her visits to his grave. What she did was to discover that she, Mary, inconspicuous woman of the house, was capable of making decisions and managing finances, getting along independently. But each night before going to bed, she would pray for the soul of her husband. It never occurred to her that they wouldn't be reunited some day. Approaching her ninetieth year, she began to lose her memory and to lose weight because she'd lost interest in her kitchen. Her hearing faded. My brother and I once had to pound on her door and bang the windows for half an hour trying to wake her up when we arrived late at night for a visit.

Her decline alarmed us. We moved her to the home in Minneapolis where we could be closer. She didn't especially concur, but there was no other choice in view of the limited options where she lived. In Minneapolis, I could see her two or three times a week, and my brother Dick, who lived in Rochester, Minnesota, visited almost as often. By then her short-term memory had disappeared. She couldn't remember today that I'd been there yesterday, although she faked it pretty guilefully. She smiled a lot in the community rooms, charming the other residents, but mostly it was a defense. She had no idea what they were saying. "Mom," I said, "there's an easy way to make life better for yourself. You'll be able to talk and hear all day." I bought a hearing aid for her.

She found six reasons why it wouldn't work. I bought new glasses for her and drew the same response. She said, "Well, I got along before without them, I can get along now." Yes, that was exasperating. But she was a little old lady digging in her feet, hanging on to the few strands of independence left to her. She was lovable but not interested much in today or tomorrow. After six months I learned that she would talk with great animation about the years in which Dick and I were children. She could quote reams of our conversations of sixty years ago, about the years in which we took piano lessons. And then we'd walk into the care home's lounge, and I'd play for a few minutes. A new color and vitality lit the frail face, and she must have happily regressed herself sixty years to the scenes where she walked around the house with a wooden spoon while I practiced, ready to wrap my knuckles if I corked off.

Would she remember the Lord's Prayer?

Not long ago, I said, "Mom, let's pray together." She looked startled. We had not done that since I was a child. And then she said, "Yes, I'd like that." She made the sign of the cross and clasped her hands together, her face close to mine. I began. "Our father, who art in heaven . . ." I tensed up for a moment. If she couldn't remember my visit of yesterday, how was she going to remember the words of a prayer?

She joined her voice with mine: "Hallowed be thy name, thy kingdom come, thy will be done . . ."

Her voice was strong and clear to the finish. It didn't miss a syllable.

She'd said that prayer a million times from childhood to her First Communion, to her wedding, every night, every Sunday morning for eighty years, at her husband's funeral service, and into her infirmity.

How was she going to forget one word of it?

When we finished, her cheeks were damp. She smiled and hugged me and said, "Son, that was beautiful. I feel much better."

It was beautiful because the prayer had brought her back to the two invincible truths remaining in her life, the love of her children and the trust in her God.

At the age of ninety, feeble and with most of her memory in shreds, she was still—without realizing it—teaching her children.

Most of the old thornbushes that got me all bloodied up in the search for God have now thinned out. The intellectual and emotional turmoils it got me into no longer trouble me much. I once read passages in the Bible that left me either puzzled or appalled. Many of those passages still baffle me. In fact, I will not and cannot believe some of them. What's different today is that I no longer find this to be cause for much sweat or consternation. So some of what I read in the Bible doesn't make sense to me. Does that mean (a) there is no sense to it or (b) if I decide there's no sense to, let's say, the story of Adam and Eve and the serpent, do I have to tell myself, "The whole business is make-believe, so good-bye, God?"

I happen to believe Adam and Eve and the serpent are inventions. I also think there's an outside chance I might be wrong. I also think my belief in God, the something great and good that's beyond me, hardly depends on a literal acceptance of the Adam and Eve story.

Does that make Genesis a fiction?

Is there anybody within earshot with enough gall to claim the power to distinguish fact from fiction here? Let's take the whole spectrum of spiritual experience and the mountains of literature that scrutinize it and the players—God, Moses, the Flood, the Red Sea splitting, Jesus Christ, the angels, the devil, the Virgin Mary, the Gospel writers, and the rest of the cast of thousands. How much of it, or them, do we include under the canopy of faith? Talking about God and the prospective hereafter is the biggest unregulated free-for-all in the world. Anybody can jump in. Nobody can be overruled, because there are no rules. You don't have to bring proof. For almost all of the argument, there is no proof. The Bible is the conventional arbiter, and if you need speed-of-light inspiration, you can now bring it up in seconds on the CD-ROM. But where is there a fact-check key that tells you what parts are hearsay or what parts must absolutely be accepted to make you part of the pilgrimage? Consider all those centuries that span the Bible stories, the multiplicity of the languages in which they were written and re-written, the conflicting cultures in which the authors wrote? What parts are plain license and imagination by the authors? Who were the actual authors and who was there on the scene to log all of those gripping quotes from God and Jesus Christ? And how much of it has been distorted or invented through the centuries by the waves of revisionists and now by the politically correct referees?

The answer, of course, is that nobody knows.

Which is why it's helpful and I'd think mandatory to bring large supplies of faith and a generous editing eye when you examine the venerated old book. At least it is for me. Hard-crust defenders argue that every syllable in it is divinely authorized. I don't believe that. If it's true, God needs a new editor. Most of the crustier ones concede that you can't take the Bible literally in all of its revelations and have to look on it as literature as well as disclosed truth. If they're correct, how *do* you take it?

The fencing is endless. I don't find that especially disrupting. In fact, the verbal brawling it's provoked is, for me, one of the alluring parts of prowling the Bible. Let's say your spiritual life has taken a significant turn. Let's say mine has.

It's then doubly absorbing to plow into the Bible for some useful clues into who God is and what God is up to. Those clues sometimes come blurred to me. So do the profiles of God. Here is the God of Exodus:

> You shall not bow down to [idols] or worship them; for I the Lord your God am a jealous God, punishing children for the iniquity of parents, to the third and the fourth generation of those who reject me, but showing steadfast love to the thousandth generation of those who love me and keep my commandments.

A jealous God. A vengeful God who lays the wood to innocent children for the sins of the parents.

I don't know about that God. Why would an omnipotent God, the creator of all, be jealous?

And is that what he really said?

At other times he is a rampaging God, flooding the world or launching pestilence. Maybe that was God, setting the boundaries early and making statements. If it was, we have defused God's temper considerably for the church bulletin boards of today, to say nothing of a creating a more congenial God for our bumper stickers.

Today God is love. God forgives. God is in the smile of your first grandchild. God is an immortal good neighbor, our confidant and our shelter.

This notion of God is obviously easier for the therapists to handle and probably gets the same high ratings from the sinners. Either way, this apparent split personality of God as reflected in biblical chronicles no longer gives me grounds for insomnia. The scriptures have increasingly become a deepening mine for exploration for me. They open up small tunnels of mystery where I like to stroll with eyes wider than they used to be and a mind that has largely made its peace with the Bible's puzzlements. I don't demand or expect literal truth in every sentence. I expect to be motivated. In random readings I expect to find my faith reinforced, and that often happens.

About the spasms of skepticism, I don't harbor much guilt today. If you've emerged from the same kind of spiritual fog I've experienced, you may have arrived at the same level of ease with the Bible's riddles. One of God's gifts to humanity, after all, was the option to exert a will and a freedom to inquire and, I suppose, the right to be wrong.

So I look at the Bible in part as extraordinary literature, still urgent, still entertaining. I look at it as a tantalizing resource to inform my wanderings through faith, honing my curiosities. Through all of the centuries of literature, for example, I think the old man summarizing his experience in Ecclesiastes still offers one of the most lyrical insights we will find into the rhythms of life, in all its wonder and its grief, and it's a thrill to speak the words aloud:

> For everything there is a season, and a time for every
>   matter under heaven:
> a time to be born, and a time to die;
> a time to plant, and a time to pluck up what is planted;
> a time to kill, and a time to heal;
> a time to break down, and a time to build up;
> a time to weep, and a time to laugh;
> a time to mourn, and a time to dance;
> a time to throw away stones, and a time to gather stones
>   together;
> a time to embrace, and a time to refrain from embracing;
> a time to seek, and a time to lose;
> a time to keep, and a time to throw away;
> a time to tear, and a time to sew;
> a time to keep silence, and a time to speak;
> a time to love, and a time to hate;
> a time for war, and a time for peace.

A time for peace. And in our personal lives, when is the time for peace? For me, when is the time for peace? It is the time when I see my resentments and my demeaning pettiness and absurdities and try to understand why I pursued them, when I recognize my vanities and fears and self-interest for what they are instead of the false colors I gave them, when I see both my weakness and worth and try to put them into some kind of recognizable canvas. It's a time when I understand my mortality, but less fearfully, because I am now closer to being whole with God.

The writer of Ecclesiastes puts us nearer that peace, if we will allow him. His is a wistful testimony, sometimes sweet, sometimes remorseful and sardonic, regretting the mistakes of self-indulgence and of a life often too distant from God.

"I denied myself nothing my eyes desired; I refused my heart no pleasure. My heart took delight in all my work, and this was the reward for all my labor. Yet when I surveyed all that my hands had done and what I had toiled to achieve, everything was meaningless, a chasing after the wind; nothing was gained under the sun. Then I turned my thoughts to consider wisdom and also madness and folly. . . . I saw that wisdom is better than folly, just as light is better than darkness . . ."

It is, when it puts a beacon on a road to a serenity that for most of us is the marker for godliness. Where else will you find a more beautiful and compelling creed for human behavior than Jesus Christ's Sermon on the Mount: "Blessed are the merciful . . . blessed are the meek . . . blessed are the peacemakers." Where is there a more gentle and more perceptive description of true love than Paul talking to the Corinthians: "Love is patient, love is kind. It does not envy, it does not boast, it is not rude, it is not self-seeking, it is not easily angered, it keeps no records of wrongs. Love does not delight in evil but rejoices with the truth. . . . Love never fails."

It does not fail when it totally submerges self. In the face of fear and the unknown, where else will you find the comfort that David gives us in the 23rd Psalm?

And yet it wasn't until I visited Israel in 1997 that the 23rd Psalm, the story of Ruth in the Old Testament, and Jesus' journey to Jerusalem were for me suddenly clothed with the fabric of reality and then a wonder that words alone couldn't create, that meshed my imagination with my senses.

We drove a narrow road from Jericho to Jerusalem, paved

but seldom used by motorists who prefer the highway. Beyond the oasis of Jericho lies a desert canyon that is wild and lonely, the chasm of the Wadi Qelt. Before you reach it you pass through the oasis, which is the land of milk and honey where the Jews emerged from the wilderness. Above its groves of palms and date trees and sycamores lifts the desert mountain where, by tradition, Jesus endured his temptation and forty-day fast. And beyond is the chasm, carved by water, wind and time. Above it, the old Roman road from Jericho to Jerusalem—the road Jesus walked—winds along the desolate sand slopes.

The spreading shadows of the late afternoon filled the gorge, deepening its austerity and, it seemed, cloaking its secrets. Even in the twentieth century, the place looked forbidding and other-worldly.

"It is a place," the guide said, "that David knew. It must have been very fearsome to travel then, hostile and filled with peril."

"The Lord is my shepherd," David wrote. "I shall not want . . . He restores my soul. He leads me in right paths for his name's sake. Even though I walk through the darkest valley . . ."

The darkest valley. It might have been this valley. Here. David was suddenly vivid, almost incarnate. The darkest valley, which in some versions of the Psalms he called, "the valley of the shadow of death." Those were the shadows of the Bible. These were the shadows of the Wadi Qelt of the twentieth century. Were they the same as David's? In front of us, the blanket of shadow slowly ascended the slopes. It overtook a flock of sheep, which had found some graze in this tormented and scabrous land and were moving slowly toward the ridge, nudged by a shepherd.

And now the sight of sheep on the hill in the gloaming fused the centuries, the ages of David and Jesus and the gaping pilgrim. We were enclosed in the great circle of biblical history. It was on this rude road on the sand slopes below us where Jesus walked to Jerusalem from Galilee, the same road where the Good Samaritan tended to a traveler robbed and left for dead.

The land was silent and seemed unforgiving. But it was also magnetic. You could not stand there in sight of Jesus' road to Jerusalem and David's shadows without being enveloped by the images and sensations and the ghosts of the thousands of years in which humanity has sought God, on this turf, slaughtered for God and been slaughtered for God, on this turf. It has coveted peace in God's name, and still aimlessly searches for that peace, on this turf, refusing to release hatreds that will not tolerate peace.

It does not mean that peace is impossible. The road to Jerusalem expanded the Bible for me. It was now more than testament and a million citations and bound leather. The Bible was now a place I could see and feel, the breeze of the Judean desert whipping sand into my face. Its characters seemed now at hand.

I know the Bible only in patches and phrases. I didn't know much about Ruth. In a wood-carving shop in Bethlehem, I stopped at a shelf whose wares included a figure carved in olive wood. The figure was of a young woman carrying a basket in one hand and a goose under her other arm. Her face was lovely and faintly weary yet filled with purpose. I asked a man nearby, evidently connected with the store, if he could tell me who was the woman in the sculpture.

"I did the carving," the artist said. "Do you know the story of Ruth?"

The carver was a balding man with a slight paunch, serious but talkative. He could have been an Arab, Jew, Palestinian, Palestinian Christian, Islamic Arab. In the Bethlehem of today, all affiliations are possible. I knew the story of Ruth dimly. He knew far more. He was a woodcarver and a trader, but to me now he took on a new identity as he talked. Here in the now bustling, commerce-driven city where Jesus Christ was born in a barn 2,000 years ago, the carver became a minstrel out of the ages, escorting me back into the times before Solomon, before David.

Ruth, he said, was a woman who lived in the land of Moab on the eastern side of the Jordan. Elimelech and his wife, Naomi, migrated there from Bethlehem because of a famine in Judah. Both sons married Moabite women. Within a few years Elimelech and the sons all died, widowing Naomi and her daughters-in-law. When Naomi returned to Israel, one of the young women remained in Moab, in accordance with custom. Ruth chose to stay with Naomi and accompanied her to Bethlehem. She explained why in words that have made her the personification of loyalty and commitment. I read the words in a Bible in the wood-carving shop: "Where you go, I will go; where you lodge, I will lodge; your people shall be my people, and your God my God. Where you die, I will die."

She remarried in Bethlehem. Her son became the grandfather of David, and is included in the New Testament among the ancestors of Jesus Christ.

I stared at the wood carver, marveling at his recital of all this in the middle of the city of David, and Ruth, and Jesus Christ. And then I looked into the face of Ruth, the woman of loyalty, and thanked the wood-carver for her history—and now mine.

Hers is a lifting story. It's a piece of the Bible that you know is real and touchable. A lot, of course, can't be touchable and demands belief, which in most cases seems a fair enough bargain. Yet if I had to put a label on the Bible's book of Revelation, with all those visions of gold and trumpets and snorting horses, I'd call it essentially bunk, although immensely descriptive bunk.

But I don't have to put a label on it, so I'm spared the fierce disapproval of my grandmother's ghost. I try hard to get serious about the book of Revelation. I can't. I may be wrong, of course. If so, I don't think that means hellfire. I think it means here is one more wrongdoer who needs remedial classes in the powers of sky's-the-limit prophecy. But that is one virtue of scrabbling around in the bedrock of one's faith. Finally, you have to ask, who or what is the God I worship?

Is this God real? My answer is yes, this God is real.

So describe this God.

And when I force myself to do that, I find this God less the celestial monarch that I once pictured and closer to the American Indians' idealization of their God, often called the Great Spirit. The Indians' life was inseparably bonded with nature for centuries. For this reason their God was and is a God lovingly identified with the earth. The God of the Indians was and is the protector of nature and the power in the elements as well as the kind and knowing spirit to whom the Indian can appeal. What attracts me in that idea of God is not so much the connection with nature. What appeals to me is the translation of God into a pervasive spirit, present everywhere, always, in every niche of our lives, not necessarily controlling, rather a compassionate spirit whose presence can offer us comfort and hope.

Yet it's almost impossible to come to grips with God without attributing to God some of the human qualities we understand. To Judeo-Christians they are human qualities written large and vivid in the scriptures, making God a literal Superman, demolishing cities when he got mad, offering solace and understanding when humans seemed to need it.

I don't see God being as fickle as that. So I deep-six the idea of a raging God, a courtroom judge kind of God. Still, this God must be something more than a God of the vapors for me. Must be. You and I probably share a need. We need to give this lofty and benevolent spirit a form we can try to grasp. And when we address that need, what is it we're doing? It is we who are creating God in our image.

Well, all right. What I'm saying is that I probably wouldn't know God if I saw him. What I do know is that God is in my life. What I know is that there is something bigger, something of power and mercy and forgiveness. And when we make that acknowledgment, we try to imagine something or someone that is literally beyond imagination. We then come to the crux of all those dilemmas: We are trying to solve a mystery we are never going to solve. We are trying to discover some steady ground that will support not only our intellect but our yearning and our dreams in how we visualize the God to whom we pray. And all of that simply can't be done at the same time because our brain isn't big enough.

So what do we do?

We may as well relax and let God be God.

What was that announcement a few eons ago?

"I am."

All right, you are. My quibbling is over. I accept. But here is Jesus Christ, who is at the heart and soul of the faith I profess. Each time I read one more magazine cover story firing up the controversy over the identity of Jesus Christ, I drive myself to the wall and want to know where I stand with Jesus Christ. Was there an actual emergence from a grave, an ascension through the stratosphere, a walking on water and a raising from the dead?

When those questions surface now, my reaction is mostly spared the old psychological goulash of anguish and flusterings. There was no television 2,000 years ago and there's going to be no replay of a resurrection on split screen. What I do know about Jesus Christ is that here was a human being we call the Son of God who walked the earth 2,000 years ago. He drew followers with the force of his message and his charismatic power. Some of what he taught meshed with the orthodoxy and the law of the times; some of it was radical in insisting on equality and sacrifice. He was the way, Jesus Christ said. It wasn't going to be an easy stroll, his way. To walk it with Jesus Christ, the Son of Man, one would have to shed the greed and jealousy, vanity and fear and arrogance that put human beings at odds with God. The way was to serve those in need; the way was humility; it was to share all of our material goods; it was to seek peace and reconciliation; the way was to forgive; the way was not only to love those who deserve our love but to love those who have injured us and therefore need our love.

What I know about Jesus Christ as the Son of Man is that he preached his message without compromise and without regard for approval. He lived it in his day-to-day travels. He sat with the poor and ate with the immoral. Yes, he said, they are sinners. But who isn't? Sometimes the point of his message seemed infuriating to notions of fairness and propriety that existed then, and still exist. He told of a landowner hiring workers at different hours of the day. The workers who sweated all day got the same wages as the ones who came on an hour before closing. When the all-day sweaters grumbled, the landowner declined to negotiate. To him, they all worked as they could and were therefore equal. To the churchgoer who still scratches his head hearing that message today, the seminary-trained mind will gently intervene in the sermon and explain that this is how the grace of God works. It does not have to be equally deserved, or deserved at all.

The Jesus Christ I know as the Son of Man took risks to heal the humanity to which he spoke. He risked social ostracism by associating with the shunned, and he risked unpopularity by preaching what most ears did not want to hear. He exposed himself to danger by afflicting the comfortable. Ultimately he went to his death because his message of sacrifice and equality, and his claim to be the voice and body of redemption threatened the traditionalists, who didn't want to hear it.

This Jesus Christ as the Son of Man died in slow agony on a cross as the price for bringing that message of healing to humanity. What I know about him is that ultimately millions accepted that message, which has affected the course of the world in ways no other teaching has. Its message of service and forgiveness and generosity has acted for the profound betterment of a humanity still rent by the evils of greed and historic hatreds.

What I know about Jesus Christ as Son of Man is less of what he has brought into the world of humanity than what his message and sacrifice have ultimately brought into mine. I say ultimately because I think today I do understand the power and divinity of God's grace in a way I didn't before. It is a grace that says, simply and without strings, you are accepted. That, in turn, fosters thanksgiving. It is a grace that has quieted some of the storms in my life and eased the need for the foolish controls I tried to exert on events and people around me. It has moved me by slow and grudging increments to the idea of humility that is the beginning of reverence and comes before serenity.

That is what I know about Jesus Christ the Son of Man. It would be good and wonderful to know more. But, when I relive the scene of my mother praying at my side, praying in utter belief and in the trust of a lifetime, I don't think it's necessary to know more.

10

The Moment of Grace

When the rest of the mysteries and the human longings sift out, what's left is the one indivisible of love. It is there at the beginning of our lives, the mother's gift, a gift of God. It is something we pursue and keep redefining as long as we live, reaching for it, trying to possess it, trying to give it, but often abusing it and sometimes running from it.

With luck, it will also be there at the end. But one of the scars of my life was my subconscious insistence on keeping it at bay.

One of the windfalls of my later years was understanding why and how.

In my years of newspapering, I sometimes came upon a story of what seemed pure and unselfish love between two people. When I wrote it, I often had to struggle to keep the fog out of my eyes. I wept because I thought I saw the most profound beauty in what they shared, yet for me a beauty elusive and just beyond reach.

The story did not always have to be touched by grief, although it was often the quiet sacrifice I saw in that love that stirred both the admiration I felt and the wistfulness that usually clouded my head when I considered those two lives. They were stories that for me were always the most compelling to tell. Some of them thrilled me in their simple expression of the unconditional trust and commitment of two people who are sure in their mutual need and devotion. But those stories also were the most painful because as the years ran on, I believed I was incapable of that kind of love.

I remember spending an hour in a restaurant listening to a thirty-five-year-old woman sharing the most traumatic day of her life. Her marriage was full of action and laughs and a dozen daily gestures of off-the-wall affection. They had no secrets. They rough-housed and did nutty things with no provocation, and when they argued it was loud and quick. And when it was over there were more laughs. But he mysteriously fell ill, and went for a series of examinations. And one day he came home to tell her that it was the worst kind of cancer, inoperable, and he was going to die in a couple of months. That was the verdict. It offered no appeal. That fast. The wonderful marriage is over, and life is over. And they bawled in each others arms and they hugged each other almost to suffocation.

And then they went into the bedroom. They had cried all they could and they would speak all the necessary words tomorrow and the days afterward. But right now they had to join their lives again to declare their unbreakable oneness, and they joined their bodies and made love. Afterward, they lay together for hours, comforting each other against the pain.

These were ordinary people. I don't know if their love was extraordinary. But reflecting on it hours later, driving home, I knew it was the kind of love that had escaped me, or to be more truthful, which I had managed to escape.

I remember attending a church wedding in which the bride came to the head of the aisle in a wheelchair. She wore a lovely white bridal gown, held flowers in her lap, and had no legs. She'd lost them while swimming, when she was struck by the propeller of a motorboat driven by a man who was drunk. The accident happened a few months before she was to be married. Yet the shock of being disabled for life was not as grievous to her as the fear that it would cost her marriage. The young man said, "It doesn't matter. I love you and I want to marry you." And while they spoke their vows that evening, the young man sat on a stool beside the woman he loved, now sitting in her wheelchair. He said it was a symbol of beginning their lives as equals. Years later I met the couple again. They had children by then. They had little money. They quarreled at times under the stress and grubbed through life. But their undiminished love revealed itself in ways that could not be mistaken—how they treated each other, how they looked at each other.

Love of that strength will touch any human who witnesses it. It might have affected me even more intensely, because I kept being shadowed by the feeling that I had somehow managed to block it out of my life, to put it beyond grasp. That got to be a conviction of mine, and the regret that it generated often lingered with me beyond the close of the work day and the telling of those stories. Inevitably, it gave way to curiosity. The self-examination. What was missing? Why? I wasn't an emotional desert. My impulses and needs, I thought, would grade out as normal on most scales. The relationships that resulted in my two marriages had put me into the lives of two women of great worth and a capacity for extending love. I thought I was giving love, but when I see it now in the aftermath I recognize it as a guarded, stifled kind of love, not a love that deserved the word in its richest meaning.

Please understand that I was very fond of these people, respected them and derived much from our relationships. There were times of spontaneous mirth and of genuine sharing, and often I initiated it. There were times of intimacy. Yet in retrospect, much of what I thought was love was closer to dutiful attention, and sometimes it was well spaced at that. I gave what I thought was love when it was convenient and, being more brutal about it, when it gave me the satisfaction of meeting my half of the partnership bargain. It was not love I gave but a stunted imitation of love, deprived of its freedom to grow because of the walls in my life and because of those continuing defenses and dishonesty bred in part by my alcoholism.

Explaining those delinquencies by understanding the impact of alcoholism didn't penetrate to the core of them, though, the real source. The real source might have been my lifelong flight from the only reconciliation that would put me in touch with the most important truths of myself, seeing the best and worst of myself, and that was reconciliation with God.

There are no standard achievement tests to measure how successful I've been in coming closer to God. I don't really apply any to myself. I can only say that since that day of surrender in the country five years ago, I have rediscovered prayer and Holy Communion, and I believe. It doesn't mean I rush around speaking in tongues and look or feel consecrated. It doesn't mean I am now converted into the Mr. Congeniality of the block, or that I can now instantly rise above impatience or spurts of foolishness or spells of dejection. I'm still susceptible to the old canker sores of my old personality. It does mean that I am now quicker to admit wrong and less proud to ask for forgiveness. I think that is true because I've regained what I believe is a vital and nourishing source of strength and trust, a center. A faith.

Like thousands of alcoholics, and millions of others unconnected with alcoholism, I can now pray for help in the sharing of a burden. I don't know why we should be surprised to discover that when that simple plea is made, the burden becomes less. My vision is probably clearer, which should not be especially astounding since my brain is less cluttered and now free from the toxins of alcohol. And now I find myself in some rare and strangely relaxed times in the day when I feel alone with that stubborn and agitating pursuer who knocked down the forts of my isolation. And it is then when I feel I am closer to understanding the purity of that unselfish love I have witnessed in others.

In those interludes I now recognize the self-centeredness in extending what I called love, and I then scramble back to Thomas Merton, who devoted a lifetime to trying to understand it, and to live it.

It is not enough for love to be shared," he found. "It must be shared freely. That is to say, it must be given, not merely taken. Unselfish love that is poured out upon a selfish object (a selfish person) does not bring perfect happiness, not because love requires a return or reward for loving but because it rests in the happiness of the beloved. The only true peace is found in selfless love. Selfless love consents to be loved self-lessly for the sake of the beloved. In so doing, it perfects itself.

If you're going to love, Merton is saying, you don't want to think about what that love is doing for you but what it does for the one you love. Such a love, he is saying, has only one good, and that is the good of the one to whom you are giving it: "Love seeks its whole good in the good of the beloved, and to divide that good would be to diminish love."

That has the look of an impossible standard to impose on fallible human beings. These are people who have to worry about the heating bills and the car payments and how do you make mutually ecstatic sex part of the night's program when both come home from the office wrung out and hauling computer spreadsheets for three meetings tomorrow. Is it a standard beyond reach?

It is a very tough standard, an ideal. But it is also an ideal that some people have managed to make the cornerstone of their lives. I don't think you'd get Merton or those who have known this kind of love to claim that it means two people staring adoringly at each other, past the television set and the heating bills, and doing it for hours. That is caricature. But this is life. What it means is two people understanding the kinks and the briars in the other and accepting them. They accept them because love doesn't demand perfection and might, in fact, be intimidated by it. It means two people whose trust in each other is secure and does not demand validation. It means two people who know each other well enough and share their lives gracefully enough to allow the other the freedom to walk separately when that seems right and necessary.

If that comes close to defining unselfish love between two people, it's probably true that many of us have not experienced it, or not allowed ourselves to experience it. Thousands, however, have. It's not a golden grail requiring a superhuman purity to bring into one's life. And if we haven't, and the years are advancing, can we tell ourselves there's still time?

I think we can.

If we didn't think we can, then the idea of redirecting one's self from the oblivion of a life without the illumination of belief, without its buoyancy, doesn't track. You don't have to be Pollyanna or a spouter of feel-good proverbs to know that you can make yourself better by making yourself less, by lowering the pickets of your pride and softening the core of your absorption with yourself. Your instincts can tell you that. But there is one thing more that can expand the worth in our lives and our receptivity to something better.

The gift of grace, I think, eventually comes to all of us. Sometimes we have trouble identifying it, trouble actually accepting it. If in fact we have come closer to God, if we've allowed God to overtake us, it may be because we have learned to recognize the grace of God. Maybe we can now define it in a way that makes sense in our lives, however theologians define it. Grace to me is God's simple and transfiguring benediction, his love, his acceptance. It brings beauty into our lives, tenderness. It comforts us in our disorder. It can inform our lives with a power of revelation that humanity's wisdom cannot. It is given with no hooks attached. It says, "I love you." It is the bounty of God, available to all, the sinner and the candidate saint, the thief in the night and the nun in the convent. It goes alike to the martyr and the brute. It is, as my friend the bishop will tell you, "God picking you up each morning, dusting you off, and breathing his love into your veins."

Can we accept that idea? A restoring gift, ours? We don't have to deserve. We don't even have to be grateful? That's a head full. But so is the whole confounding mystery of life and creation, God and struggling humans, their relationship and does it ever end? About the bestowal of this grace—and how or if the beneficiary ought to respond—people who are devout or dogmatic or both have chewed up millions of words arguing.

We can argue about it or wonder. What we probably can't deny are the times when we feel it. We may call it by a different name: luck, the gift of nature, serendipity, humanity. It can be one of those tidal-wave transformations. More likely it is the continuing gift of forgiveness, the daily gift, since I don't suppose you can get by with being pardoned once in your life any more than you can hope to commit sin just once in your life. But the grace I have come to feel or come now to understand better is not confined to the idea of being absolved. More likely I will feel it an hour or a moment when I am touched by a loveliness in the earth, or in music, or in the face of a stranger, or in the thoughtfulness of a friend trying to heal my pain.

Where did the beauty I see and hear or the unexpected generosity I receive come from, after all? Late in the day several years ago I walked along the trail from our campsite beside a cascading stream in the Himalayas, a few minutes before supper. The forested slopes beneath the great mountains were strewn with huge boulders carried down by the glaciers. One of them lay beside the trail. It was forty to fifty feet high but presented an inviting flat surface on top. I scrambled up to a place where I could sit to watch marvelous streamers of sunlight pouring through the pinnacles and glazing the snowfields of Thamserku, a stunning mountain a few miles from Everest. The rock where I took up this impromptu vigil was warm to the hands in the setting sun. I offered a brief prayer of thanks to be allowed a rare moment like this, and then dozed for a few minutes. I woke to voices and footsteps beneath. A Sherpa farmer and his wife were walking the trail to their home on the dirt plateau five hundred feet above the river that flowed beneath the wood bridge they had to cross. A boy about five walked behind them.

They were carrying tools and sacks from their potato field on our side of the river. The boy looked up and saw what must have been a spectacle for him—a visitor from the west, maybe the first he'd seen, wearing the colorful and expensive hiking clothes the westerners often bring to the Himalayan trek.

The boy stared at me with those wonderful brown saucer eyes beneath his flopping hair, and I stood to wave. He stared some more, and timidly returned my wave. When he got to the bridge, he waved more aggressively. So did I. When they reached the other side of the bridge, he grew more excited with each wave, his parents oblivious to all of this. At each turn of the trail's switchbacks up the slope, through the rhododendron trees he repeated the thrashings of his arms, and I responded. The exchange of all of that amiable energy almost got to be a contest. At the top of the hill, his mother finally had a chance to observe the action. She looked across the gorge to find out who and what was the object of the boy's exertions, and then lowered her head to speak to him. He then turned to me, placed this hands together, fingertips together as in prayer, and brought them to his lips. I couldn't hear, of course, but I knew what he must have been saying, and I returned the gesture. The word the boy spoke was *namaste* (pronounced *nah-mah-stay*). In Nepalese, it translates into "I salute the God who lives within you." It is the loveliest word I know. It makes a day worthwhile knowing there is such a word and thought.

And here it was being exchanged between a poor child, living in the potato fields of the high Himalaya mountains, and an aging Westerner who had come back to these mountains both for the excitement of them and the sustenance of them. What I found in one unforeseen click of time was a connection that I will never forget. It seemed to harmonize the lives of two strangers, living a half world apart, separated by cultural chasms. For a few minutes our lives and our yearnings were joined. The sun poured through the boy's mountains and the rhododendron trees and touched both his lips and those of the aging man on the rock, the two of them united in a simple prayer honoring the same God they worshiped by different names.

I believe there was a grace in that moment.

I know there was. And we received it in a way so precious that it invited a deeper understanding of that solidarity of which worship is so much a part, the community of pilgrims uniting their voices and their hopes. The community is larger than we realized, it is universal, and it somehow immortalizes those hopes.

So where does it or can it take us, this grace of God? The place may not necessarily be wonderful. The place I have found is filled with the recognition of what's wrong with me, and it is roughened with pain and regret and hindsight. Yet those have been the forerunners of a fulfillment deeper than what I have felt before. The healing and, yes, the joy make small advances each day. Most of the tumult in my life has receded. Like my grizzled friend, the battered reverend, I don't know where all this leads. Yet looking at the place where I am today, comparing it with where I was before the healing began, I can honestly say, if that's all there is, then I am content.

But I doubt that's all there is, because each day when I rise in the morning I tell myself, "You are loved, you are forgiven, and you have something to give."

The thought makes the coming day vital and good, and gives me peace.